bathrooms

bathrooms

Vinny Lee

photography **Chris Everard**

RYLAND
PETERS
& SMALL

London New York

Designer **Sally Powell**

Senior editor **Henrietta Heald**

Managing editor **Sian Parkhouse**

Location research manager **Kate Brunt**

Location researcher **Sarah Hepworth**

Production manager **Meryl Silbert**

Art director **Gabriella Le Grazie**

Publishing director **Alison Starling**

Stylist **Lucy Gibbons**

To AWJ, my companion in life's bubbly tub

First published in the United Kingdom in 2000
by Ryland Peters & Small
Kirkman House
12–14 Whitfield Street
London W1T 2RP
www.rylandpeters.com

10 9 8 7 6 5 4 3

Text © Vinny Lee 2000
Design and photographs
© Ryland Peters & Small 2000

Printed and bound in China

ISBN 1 84172 081 X

A CIP record for this book is available from
the British Library.

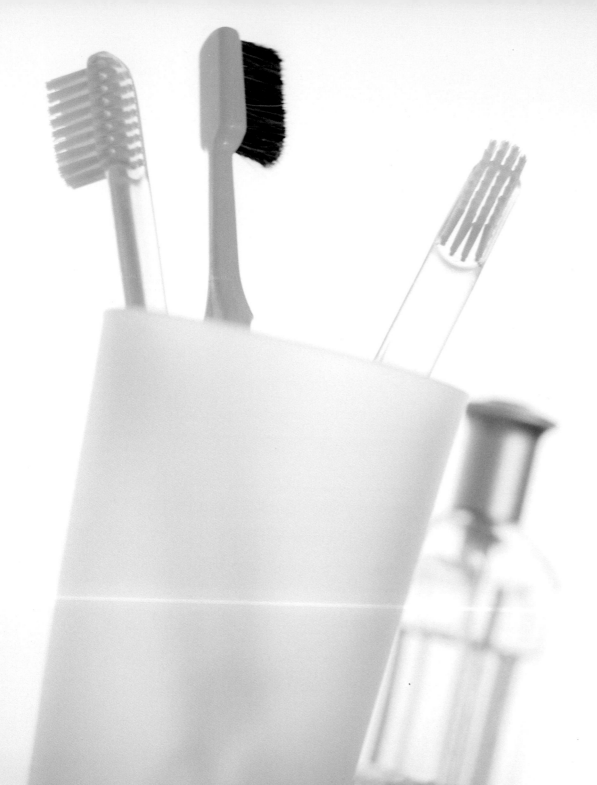

introduction

There is more to bathing than simply getting clean. As well as giving you time to yourself, it can be therapeutic, reviving for jaded spirits, calming and relaxing. The room in which these activities takes place is one of the most intimate spaces in the house, where decoration and design can enhance the pleasures enjoyed within.

The act of bathing, rather than just washing, was popular among the ancient Egyptians, Greeks and Romans. The Romans built large communal baths, which included massage areas and steam rooms. However, for much of history, the pleasures of the bath were largely shunned in the West because they were associated with licentiousness and sensuality rather than cleanliness and health. Times have changed. These days, especially in summer, some people shower two or three times a day to refresh and cool themselves.

Direct water supply and drainage became more widely available in prosperous Western countries at the end of the 19th century. After the introduction of Britain's first Public Health Act in 1875, clean running water was piped to most houses and efficient sewage systems took waste away. The health benefits of washing were also acknowledged. Although many richer households and grand hotels had bathrooms, it was not until after the Second World War that lavatories were commonly plumbed inside the house instead of out in the yard, and new homes were built with designated bathroom spaces. Until then most bathing had taken place in a portable metal hip bath, or consisted of a scrub down with a jug of water and a bowl to stand in, often in front of the kitchen range.

Early bathrooms were functional places, with linoleum on the floor and tiles or other waterproof protection around the bath. Baths were taken once a week, and hair washing became a ritual Friday night activity. Hot water – regarded as a luxury in the financially restrained times of the late 1940s and 1950s – was used sparingly. Today the bathroom

is as much part of the home as any other room, and worries about water usage are more environmental than economic. Decoration is carefully planned, and furniture and fittings are thoughtfully chosen. From the 1960s, the advent of new materials and a more adventurous aesthetic sense saw bathroom styles and colours change considerably.

Among the many new ideas to be gleaned from cultures where bathing has always been a part of daily life is the belief that bathing should never be rushed. It should be a long, luxurious ritual that may involve two, three or more processes. Where possible, it should also be a communal and sociable affair. In the Scandinavian sauna, for example, the participants sit or lie on wooden benches. Traditionally, when they have perspired enough, they roll in the snow outside or hose themselves down with cold water to close the pores of the skin that have been opened by the warmth. The heat of the sauna is enhanced by a small open brazier of hot coals onto which water is poured. Essences such as eucalyptus or pine can also be added to mingle with the steam. Some people scrub themselves with birch twigs, which are abrasive and also have a mild scent.

The practice of varying temperatures while bathing, found both in the sauna and the Turkish bath, can be traced back to Roman times, when the public baths were divided into three sections: the tepidarium, the caldarium and the frigidarium – temperatures varied between warm and icy cold, so that the ambience changed from balmy and relaxing to bracing and stimulating, benefiting both the skin and the circulation. This experience can easily be replicated in the modern bathroom. Sitting in a well-sealed shower cabinet with hot water pumping out of the shower head, you will be exposed to raised levels of temperature and steam; with the turn of a dial, the water can be changed to cold, which will do much to invigorate the systems of the body.

1
first principles

planning and design

fitting and installing

THE FIRST PROPER BATHROOMS EMERGED IN LATE VICTORIAN TIMES – SMALL

FUNCTIONAL ROOMS NOT MUCH WIDER THAN THE WIDTH OF THE BATH WITH THE

LAVATORY AT ONE SIDE, AND RARELY LONGER THAN THE LENGTH OF THE BATH WITH

SPACE FOR A HANDBASIN AT ITS FOOT. DECORATION WAS SIMPLE AND MUNDANE

– WITH WHITE OR OFF-WHITE STANDARD-SHAPED ENAMEL BATHS AND CLASSIC

CERAMIC BASINS. THE BATHROOM OF THIS ERA WAS ENTIRELY UTILITARIAN, AND

THERE WAS LITTLE SPACE FOR MORE THAN ONE PERSON TO WASH AT A TIME.

Today's bathroom is an increasingly important room – and planning and creating a bathroom that fulfils

all your needs is a demanding task. While still primarily a place in which to bathe or shower, a bathroom

may double as an exercise area, a dressing room or even a laundry – requiring space to accommodate

a rowing machine or an aerobic step, cupboards and chests of drawers, or a washing machine and a

drier with their associated ducts and pipes. Medicines and cosmetics are often stored and applied or

administered in a bathroom; beauty treatments are carried out there; and for those indulging in a relaxing

soak it may also be a place simply to listen to music, read a book or sip a glass of wine.

More and more people are installing second bathrooms or additional washing facilities in their homes.

A family with young children who must be ready for school at the same time as their parents leave for

work may find a second bathroom a necessity rather than a luxury – unless, for example, handbasins are

installed in the bedrooms to ease demand on the main bathroom.

Modern technological developments mean that showers and separate lavatories can be plumbed into

wardrobe and cupboard spaces or into the often useless sloping area under a staircase. En suite bathrooms

are also popular, and some people sacrifice a spare bedroom in favour of a spacious extra bathroom.

Whether you are re-doing an existing bathroom, making a new one or contemplating adding a secondary washing facility, good preparation is essential. Care in the early stages will save you time, money and headaches later on. Even if you are working with an architect or interior designer, it is useful to have established in your own mind what you hope to achieve in the finished room, and an awareness of the wide range of options available in equipment, surfaces and decoration will give you the confidence to make balanced and informed decisions.

One way of keeping up to date with technological advances is to read some recent issues of specialist bathroom magazines. Bath showrooms are also a useful point of reference – they often have display models that you can see in action. New bath shapes and sizes, shower heads and water heaters, finishes, materials and lighting are also regularly coming onto the market. If you collect manufacturers' brochures giving sizes and measurements, you will build up an invaluable file of technical information.

Safety should be addressed at each stage of design, planning, fitting and installation of a bathroom, for it is a place where you are potentially very vulnerable, where your skin is unprotected and the dangers from sharp objects, hot pipes, slippery mats and hard surfaces are ever present.

planning and design

When planning a new bathroom, altering an old one or installing a new washing facility, such as a cloakroom or shower room, start by working out how much space you have to play with, and then make a list of your aims and priorities.

If you are handy with a pencil and squared paper, you might try drawing a floor plan. If not, don't worry – many large bathroom shops offer a computer design service that will enable you to see how various styles of bathroom suite can be arranged within the confines of your room. But you will need to sketch a rough outline of the room, with door and window positions indicated, and to take measurements of the distances between the door and the corner of the room, the window height, and so on, so that the computer can be programmed with accurate figures.

When you are calculating the cost of the building work and fixtures, remember to reserve some of your budget for decorating. A bathroom can be one of the most satisfying rooms to decorate. Its relative smallness means that it can be finished more quickly than a larger room, and you can introduce schemes and materials that might be regarded as too costly or flamboyant for a more public space.

Identifying your needs

The next stage is to decide exactly what you require. Is the aim to create a main bathroom or an additional facility to satisfy competing demands? Can the various lavatory and washing needs be divided between two spaces or more? How many people will be using the facilities?

Young children, elderly people and people with disabilities have special requirements. For example, anyone who is wheelchair-bound needs more space to manoeuvre, and grab rails to help with getting in and out or up and down. Wall-hung basins and lavatories are useful for disabled people because the lack of a pedestal gives easier and closer access to the bowl. Non-slip flooring is of crucial importance for those whose youth or frailty means that they are unsteady on their feet. Bathing can be especially

Simple shapes can look dramatic in plain, uncluttered surroundings. This graceful curved handbasin and simple wall-mounted spout are practical but also attractive. When planning and fitting out your bathroom, start with less and build up to more, rather than the other way round.

Left **Provide plenty of easily accessible storage and aim to keep surfaces free of clutter. This strategy will not only make it easier to wipe the surfaces clean but will also add to the aesthetic appearance of the room, especially if it is a modern streamlined design.**

Above and right **Large tiles can be used to create an illusion of space. They are now available in a variety of materials that were once confined to outdoor settings – for example, slate, lime-stone and sandstone, which have inherent waterproof properties and can be finished with a smooth or polished surface.**

challenging for elderly people or those with conditions such as arthritis – although the warmth and relaxing effect of a bath can bring great benefits, the effort of bathing may be a strain. One inexpensive solution is a bath board – a simple but specially designed benchlike seat that lies across the top rim of the bath; this device is not altogether satisfactory, however, because the body of the bather is not immersed.

Also on the market are retractable bands which act as a hoist seat – they can be automatically and mechanically raised and lowered as needed. Hydraulic chairs with hand-operated controls are among the easiest to use but can be expensive to buy and install. Walk-in baths that offer a combination of bath and shower are also widely available. The walk-in bath is a hybrid of a shower cabinet and a small bath with a built-in seat. You enter by a low door at the front which closes tightly to create a deep but upright bathing space.

Bathrooms designed for those with impaired physical ability do not need to be clinical or ugly. Wall grips can be disguised as soap dishes and low-height baths can look elegant rather than specially plumbed in for a geriatric patient. Thermostatic filler controls on the bath can be pre-set to a maximum 38°C or a temperature that the bather feels comfortable with, so that there is no risk of scalding. These controls are also ideal for bathrooms used by children because the water temperature can be set below the level at which they might sustain a scald.

Children and teenagers

Children, especially babies and toddlers, need to be kept warm during and after bathing, so adequate heating is important. The bath should have a non-slip base and be easily accessible for people who are supervising washing and bathtime. Baths with built-in seats to one side are ideal for toddlers, who can sit there comfortably and be showered or sponged down, rather than sitting or lying vulnerably on the base of a large bath. Baths for children should be filled only to a few centimetres so that their faces are well above the water level if they slip or slide in the bath. Never leave a baby or toddler alone in the bathroom.

If your home is on two or more levels, it is a bonus to have a separate lavatory and basin on a level other than where the bathroom is located. Such an arrangement can save time and effort for adults, and in a household with small children having a lavatory on the same floor of the house as the main living rooms, kitchen and/or play area takes away the need to carry babies and supervise tots up and down stairs and makes toilet training less of a trial.

Teenagers may feel shy about their changing bodies and prefer not to share the bathroom with others. They are also notorious for spending an inordinate length of time in the bathroom – a strange turn of events from their childhood, when bathtime was often the most hated part of the day. To resolve this situation you could install a shower in the bedroom or in a room other than the main bathroom.

Exercise and meditation

Keep-fit and exercise facilities can also be located in the bathroom if there is space for them. After rigorous exercise it is very satisfying to be able to step straight into a cooling and cleansing shower or warm bath. Floor and aerobic exercises can take place on a soft padded mat or with weights, but an exercise machine with electrical parts should be kept well away from any contact with water, and the room should be well ventilated to prevent the machine from getting damp. If you are thinking about putting this type of machine in your bathroom, consult the manufacturer or an accredited electrician.

The simple, clean and private environment of the bathroom can also be conducive to practising meditation and yoga. When you are physically cleansed and in a relaxed frame of mind, you may find that allowing time to clear your mind is also beneficial. A lightly padded mat can make lying

on the floor more comfortable, or – if you have enough room to spare – a futon-style day bed or chaise would be a luxurious addition. If you are leaving upholstered furniture, padded mats or cushions in the room for any length of time, ensure that the ventilation is effective enough to extract the damp and steam generated by showering or bathing, so that the fabrics do not become damp and mouldy.

If your dream is to have private and uninterrupted access to your own bathroom, you may need either to knock through a wall to a next-door room or re-use existing space such as a fitted wardrobe, an archway or a recess. One attraction of an ensuite bathroom is that it is reserved primarily for your and your partner's use and enjoyment.

Assessing the options

When you have a general idea of the facilities you wish to install, start collecting brochures and catalogues and visiting specialist showrooms. There are numerous makes and brands of fixture, and developments in technology and mass production mean that there is a wider choice than ever of affordable bathrooms. Once regarded as elitist, Jacuzzis and other devices that deliver water in the form of therapeutic massage jets are now easier to find.

After surveying the market and establishing the costs, colours and installation requirements of various items, you can start more detailed planning. Discuss your plans with a builder, carpenter, electrician and/or plumber, depending on the scale of the job, and get their input and ideas, as well as estimated costs. The styles and shapes of fixtures on the market range from the traditional to the ultra-modern – from countertop or

Above **Double basins can be useful in a bathroom used regularly by two people, especially in the morning rush to get ready for work. The scheme shown here brings together hard and soft elements. Cool steel basins are set in a rich warm cherrywood surface with matching splashback, which also echoes the colour and material used for the floor.**

Left and opposite page, near right **Where space is limited, one solution is to combine some facilities by installing, for example, a shower over a bath or a lavatory with a bidet-style shower attachment. Hairwashing can be made easier by wall-mounting the waterspout above a handbasin.**

Opposite page, top **As long as your bathroom is not overlooked, curtains or blinds may be needed only to give you a feeling of privacy at night, when it is dark outside. Otherwise, if you have a view, make the most of it. Here a mirrored wall is used to enhance the impact of a wonderful vista of the New York City skyline, as well as to provide a waterproof setting for a shower.**

Opposite page, far right **En suite bathrooms are increasingly popular. Among their advantages is the fact that you can get dressed immediately after washing without having to go to another room.**

dropped-in vanity units to small hand-rinse sinks for cloakrooms, and from reproductions of traditional lavatories with the cistern wall-mounted high above the bowl and flushed by a handle on a metal chain to the sleekest bowl with concealed cistern. Baths come in various materials from rigid acrylic to pressed steel, and from the classic rolltop to the standard oblong, as well as the sculpted corner bath.

Try not to be overwhelmed by the choice, but be rigorous about dismissing those items you are not certain about and keep notes about those with outstanding appeal. Budgetary and space constraints will help to whittle down the choice.

Study carefully the dimensions and scale of each item. A corner bath might appear to save space but may in fact take up more room than a standard bath. In some cases the actual bathing space within the surround may be the same as, if not smaller than, a standard bath, but the curved fascia and corner panelling can mean that the bath extends farther into the room than a regular oblong bath would.

There are not only a multitude of styles, colours and finishes to choose from but also modern innovations such as macerator lavatories and small-bore pumping systems. You may find the technicalities of such equipment bewildering, but take home a brochure to read at your leisure or to discuss with your plumber or builder.

Remember that, although gadgets and electronic wizardry may seem very appealing, the more items of that sort that you have installed the more there is to go wrong, and in a bathroom – where any electrical fittings and wiring must be safely concealed – it could be difficult to get access to them without having to disrupt other objects in the room.

Above **In a large indulgent bathroom the impact of the fixtures can be softened by setting them against painted walls and textured floor coverings. These classic handbasins with raised curved surrounds have a period feel which complements the chest of drawers, the towel ring and the simple circular mirrors.**
Right **Some fixtures resemble items of furniture, with a flat, table-like top, and legs rather than a pedestal base.**

Macerator lavatories are generally efficient but it is unwise to rely on them as a main or sole outlet. The main lavatory in the house should be plumbed through to the main waste pipe to cope with the majority of the daily output, but the macerator is an ideal back-up or secondary facility. You have to be vigilant about the type of waste that is disposed of in a macerator lavatory because of the restrictions in the pipe size and flow. Most manufacturers of this type of fixture specify that, along with normal bodily waste, only a small amount of soft lavatory paper should be disposed of in a macerator lavatory – otherwise the narrow pipes and machinery of the system are in danger of becoming clogged.

The small-bore pumping system pumps waste, on average, a distance of 50 metres horizontally and up to 4 metres vertically. This system allows lavatories, handbasins and showers to be fitted into small spaces such as lofts and attic conversions, where conventional gravity-fed plumbing has not been widely available, and into inner parts of the home where there is no direct access to the main soil pipes.

The technology applies not just to the dispersal of waste water and matter but to increasing the power of the water that is available for use in the shower. Pumps can be added to water pipes and heaters to ensure that showers installed in attics or rooftop spaces supply a decent head of spray. It is no longer necessary, as it once was, to plumb a shower into a space that is at least 4 metres lower than the overhead water tank in order to supply the downward pressure necessary to achieve a vigorous flow of water.

Matters of size

To meet the increasing demand for smaller units and fixtures that can be used in small or secondary bathrooms, manufacturers have developed ranges specifically to fit these spaces. There are small but deep baths, shower cabinets that are triangular and fit into corners, or totally enclosed tube-shaped pods with integral shower trays.

For any washing facilities in a restricted space, adequate ventilation is very important. Damp and moisture will accumulate quickly but are slow to disperse, and may cause damage in the long term unless they are efficiently expelled or ducted away.

There are small but often overlooked ways that can add precious centimetres to a room. For example, you may gain space in the dead area behind the main door to the room by hanging it so that it opens outwards rather than inwards – but make sure that you have enough space on the landing or hallway outside to allow people to pass, and check that the opened door will not block off the whole passageway.

A handbasin can be hung in such a way that it overlaps slightly with the foot of a bath – this should be done at the tap end rather than at the head end of the bath so that there is no danger of banging your head against the side. Alternatively, the foot end of a bath could be slotted in under the slope of an attic roof or under the rise of a overhead staircase. This would allow you to accommodate a full-length bath and make use of the height at one end of the bath, even though the height at the other end may be restricted.

The same approach could be applied to the cistern of a lavatory; the back of the toilet and cistern can be plumbed into an area of restricted height while the sitting or standing area in front of it is sited in a part of the room where the ceiling gradually rises to full height.

By choosing a wall-mounted handbasin rather than one that has been sunk into a vanity unit you will be able to make use of the extra inches on either side of the basin. If you are plumbing a ceramic fitment behind a door, select a rounded-corner basin rather than a square one so that the door is less likely to bang against the edge of the fixture and damage it.

Below **This old-fashioned, high-level lavatory with its raised water tank and wooden seat has a strong period character which has been reflected in the choice of decor. The walls have been wood-panelled and painted in a single, plain colour, and the floor has been clad in wood. The classic column radiator serves both as a source of heat and as a convenient towel rail.**

A standard-sized handbasin may not always be necessary. For example, in a cloakroom or spare bedroom, where rinsing hands and washing teeth are the main activities, a smaller rinse-basin may be adequate.

Even in a spacious bathroom detailed planning is important. If two people need to use the bathroom at the same time, a pair of handbasins can help to speed up the washing routine in the mornings and evenings. Individual storage cabinets installed above or below the basins mean that each person's particular toothbrush, toothpaste, deodorant and other toiletries can be kept readily to hand.

You may want to subdivide the space in a large room and give definition to separate areas – a scheme that can be enhanced by careful positioning of lighting. More permanent subdivisions can also be

introduced into a large space. For example, a purpose-built wall known as a stud wall can be constructed to enclose the area around the bath, making it cosier, and decorated to create an intimate and indulgent room within a room. Handbasins can be screened from the bath or shower enclosure by a wall of glass bricks, which will allow light to travel through them and provide a certain amount of obscurity. Glass bricks have a watery appearance and are sturdy without appearing too dense or solid.

If you are not in favour of installing a permanent surround, a simple movable screen or even a decorative shower curtain on a pole can be used to create a more snug environment. Freestanding or floating walls are a popular foil in large rooms. One side of the wall is frequently used to provide a splashback to a shower while the bath is plumbed in on the other side – so that each fixture is obscured from the other. This type of feature can create a particularly dramatic and arresting effect in minimalist bathrooms or wet rooms where the wall surfaces are covered in a single colour or finish.

In a large bathroom the lavatory and bidet may be concealed in a ventilated enclosure, so that they appear to be absent from the room. This provides privacy when the facilities are in use and also means that there is easy access to the rest of the bathroom. A faux cupboard is another discreet form of disguise – the exterior of the cupboard can be decorated so that it is almost invisible in the overall scheme of the walls.

An imaginative way to add interest to a small bathroom is to erect a partition or low wall. Often the most economical way of using space in a narrow bathroom is to arrange the fixtures according to a linear scheme, in which the bath is placed in the corner at the far end from the door, with the lavatory beside the bath and the basin at its foot. This is a rather conventional layout but, if there is enough space, it can be made less so by building a mid-height, low wall at the open end of the bath. The wall will not only contain the bathing area but also provide an extended splashback around a basin. Another low wall can be used to separate the side of the bath from the lavatory, giving more privacy to both areas.

Opposite page **Three views of the same bathroom show how circular windows and carefully placed mirrors, lights and ornaments can offset the potentially harsh effect created by the boxy, angular shapes of the bath, the basin unit and the dividing wall separating the shower enclosure from the rest of the room.** This page **In these bathrooms, by contrast, the angular lines of the fixtures have been emphasized with oblong mirrors, long slatted blinds, linear wooden decking beside the bath, a partition with square glass panels and linear towel rails.**

Adding facilities to an existing room

Some people incorporate washing facilities in a part of the house also used for other purposes. For example, the bathroom or lavatory and handbasin may be part of a utility room where laundry is done. The room will already be decorated to withstand steam, moisture and temperature variations, and much of the plumbing, pipes and wiring necessary for the installation of bathroom fixtures will be in place. There are obvious advantages to keeping washing machines and lavatories together in one area.

If you intend to install a small cloakroom with a lavatory and handbasin near an area where food is customarily prepared or eaten, planning regulations in most countries require that there is a double-ventilated

lobby between the two spaces to ensure safety and maintain good hygiene. The ventilated lobby means that there is a door in the room where the lavatory is installed, a small lobby area with adequate ventilation in between, and then another door that provides access to the second room.

Efficient ventilation is also required in a bathroom that, for example, doubles as a dressing room or is used for the storage of bedlinens and towels. To prevent these fabrics from becoming damp and eventually succumbing to mildew, it is necessary to promote vigorous circulation of air through the room. A dressing room is often located near the bathroom for convenience of use, and sometimes this can offer an unexpected

advantage, in that materials such as wrinkled silk or velvet benefit from hanging temporarily in a steamy place – this is because the warmth and moisture help to relax the fabric and encourage the creases to drop out.

Other practical considerations

There are a number of other practical matters that should be addressed in the early stages of planning a bathroom. For example, if you plan to put a cast-iron bath in an upper room, check with the builder or architect that the weight of the bath combined with the weight of the bather and the water when the bath is filled will not be too heavy for the floor to support. If there is any doubt about this, you may need to reinforce the ceiling joists of the room below to carry the load.

If you plan to install a wet room – a dedicated shower room with a graduated floor and a single water out-take – check that the weight of the tiles is not likely to create a problem, especially if you are using something as substantial as slate.

In preparation for constructing a wet room, it is necessary to ensure that the walls, floor and ceiling can be adequately waterproofed and that the waste water will be efficiently ducted away from a central plughole. This may be difficult to achieve in an upper-floor room unless you are also prepared to go to the trouble of constructing a false floor under which the piping can be laid.

Relocating existing fixtures can be more expensive than installing new ones because the old item or items will have to be disconnected before being taken elsewhere. Existing pipework may need to be closed off both internally and externally, so make allowances in your budget for this – and for having your water disconnected and tanks or pipes drained. You also need to be prepared to endure the inconvenience of spending a day or so without proper bathroom facilities.

When choosing the various items and deciding where to place them, take account of cleaning and wear and tear. You may find that one of the modern wall-hung lavatories with a concealed water cistern, known as a back-to-the-wall design, is particularly appropriate in a family bathroom. They offer easy access for cleaning around the base; there are no pedestal or niches where dust can gather, and the hidden cistern does not require to be regularly wiped down.

When planning this type of installation, remember that if the cistern is concealed behind panelling, access to it will be necessary in case of plumbing problems – so you need to ensure that there is a removable section within the panelling. The more ornate and delicate bathroom ware such as glass basins and brass bathtubs, are best suited to an adult's en suite bathroom, where they will not suffer as much wear and tear as they would in a communal family bathroom.

You may also want to think about varying the levels within a bathroom. For example, creating a step up to the bath can give a feeling of luxury and may also be a useful way of concealing ugly or intrusive

Above The choice of materials for surface areas needs careful thought. The top priority is that any such material should be waterproof and resilient to temperature changes and steam. Stone is a naturally weather-proof material that can, with underfloor heating, be made to feel comfortable under bare feet.

Right **Stone corners or edges, such as these lining a drainage channel, should be rounded to prevent injury. This particularly applies to shelves and to bath and basin surrounds.**

Unusual building materials can also be effective in a bathroom. For example, this clear corrugated sheeting is more often found on the roofs of garden sheds and industrial warehouses than in indoor situations, but it has all the qualities required to make it a useful and intriguing cladding for a bath base and as a partition.

pipework. A 'sunken' bath does not have to be sunk into the floor – you can bring the floor up to meet it, and create the impression that the bath is a sunken bath by building steps up to the surround. The addition of this sort of feature can give a fresh look and feel to an existing bathroom without involving you in the trouble and expense of having to replumb or relocate the bath.

fitting and installing

Once you have devised a floor plan the next step
is to tackle the technical and practical elements of
installing a bathroom. You need not know everything
about wiring diagrams and plumbing regulations but
it is useful to be aware of the pros and cons of
different systems and the main safety requirements.

Far left **The slope-sided steel basin
and mirrors above it were custom-
made for this bathroom, but these
modern elements are teamed with
classic elements such as the Pietra
Santa limestone flooring and a
1930s magnifying mirror found
in a flea market.**

Below left and below **A simple spout
has been set into the surface at the**

side of the basin, rather than behind
it in the more conventional position.
This leaves the surface free in front
of the mirror, giving the person using
the basin a clearer view.

Bottom left **In this small bathroom a
tap has been fitted on the far side of
the basin from the lavatory so that it
does not intrude upon the area where
someone may wish to sit down.**

Knowing in advance about the sort
of problems that might arise can
save time and money. You should
make allowances in your building
schedule for technical hitches and
overlapping work – the kind of
thing that happens when the wiring
needs to be put in before the tiles
can be laid, or the plumber needs
to fit the taps at the same time as
the basin, which is not due to arrive
until two weeks later. Organizing
workers to come at the right time,
and for various items to be delivered
when needed, is like fitting together
the pieces of a jigsaw.

Position is not the only thing to
consider when installing the items in
a bathroom – height is important
too. For example, tall people may
find it less of a strain on the lower
back if the basin is placed at their
hip to waist height rather than at a
standard pedestal height. This may
mean either building a false base to
raise the pedestal or choosing a
basin that can be mounted on a wall or sunk into a vanity unit.

The direction in which the cupboard doors open is also worth thinking
about. If cupboard doors open out onto each other, it can be difficult to
reach the contents of the cupboard; if the doors clash with those of the
shower cabinet or the main door of the room, there may be accidents

when they are in use at the same time. If you foresee a problem, check with the supplier whether the shower is available with a door that opens in the opposite direction, or ask the carpenter whether it is feasible to hang the cupboard doors from the other side.

Acquaintance with some of the complications of installation and with a few of the more general technical terms will put you in a good position to ask relevant questions when you are buying fixtures and fittings, as well

as to talk with some authority to the people who will install them. Do not be afraid to ask questions – and before paying a deposit to a contractor make sure that you have a clear understanding of what has been agreed.

Safety

Any work involving close contact between water and electricity should be carried out by a professional, preferably someone registered with a recognized organization. Use only fixtures and fittings specifically designed for bathrooms and shower rooms. High-voltage lights should be turned on and off by means of a cord, or from a switch outside the bathroom, so that wet hands do not come in contact with the electrical outlet, but most low-voltage lighting can be operated safely from switches within the room. Light bulbs should be encased in sealed units that protect the fitting from steam and condensation. Bathroom heaters must also comply with safety regulations. Electrical appliances that use standard plugs, such as heated hair tongs, rollers and hairdryers should not be used in the bathroom. Indeed, the only sockets seen in a bathroom should be those approved for shavers and similar equipment.

If you have a shower in a bedroom, it must be at least 2.5m from any electrical socket. Any metal parts of baths, showers, pipes, taps or radiators are potentially hazardous if they make contact with a live electrical current, so they are usually connected to an earthing wire. In the event that a live current is transmitted to the fixture or appliance, the earthing wire causes the current to break before any damage is done.

Plumbing

Plumbing is another specialist job that is best done by a professional. Leaking pipes and incorrectly fitted joints and overflows can cause spills and drips which may damage walls and floors, leading to rot and even in severe cases to the loss of a floor or ceiling.

Pipes in a bathroom should be carefully positioned, and hot pipes should be lagged, insulated or covered, and if possible boxed, to keep in the heat and to prevent nearby cold-water pipes from warming up. If the hot pipes are in an area where they could be touched by bare skin, they should also be covered to prevent any burns or surprise contact.

The vogue for freestanding baths and basins means that such fixtures may be placed in the centre of a room, or at some distance from the wall, so that water pipes have to be laid across the room from the wall where they are normally fed in. To accommodate this type of plumbing, it is necessary to lift the floor – while it is up, you could take the opportunity to lay down some insulation or cladding to prevent any heat marks discolouring the ceiling below and to keep the heat of the water in the pipes. It may also be a good time to put down underfloor heating.

If you are installing a whirlpool or spa bath, choose a system with rigid pipework, which allows the water to drain away completely. Flexible pipework sometimes sags, allowing the dirty water to settle in the pipes

Above **Wall-mounted taps and spouts should be carefully installed, and the stone or tiles in which they are set need to be professionally cut.**
Right **Steel used to be thought of as an almost exclusively industrial** material. **It was used in washing facilities only in such institutions as army barracks, but in the early 21st century it has become increasingly accepted as a practical and chic material for fixtures in the home.**

Right and opposite page **From the wide choice of taps and spouts try to pick a style that not only complements the design of the fixtures but also fits comfortably with the shape and size of your hands. The configurations of taps, waste outlets and plugs also vary. If you are not placing the spout in the conventional place – in the centre back of the basin – it is important to ensure that the flow of water has direct and easy access to the waste outlet and does not cause splashing.**

and to be pumped back into the bath next time it is used. Also, if the bath remains unused for some time, the dirty water may become stagnant and start to smell.

Before installing an old or antique bath or handbasin, check whether it has an overflow outlet – some old baths and basins were filled and emptied by hand. If there isn't an overflow in your antique bath, you may want to have one added when the bath is plumbed in.

Tiling and sealing

Water will seep anywhere it can, through cracks and openings of any size, so it is important to seal surfaces that are prone to splashing and those that are in regular contact with moisture. If water seeps behind a bath and settles on wooden floorboards, they may become saturated and in time start to rot; the same applies to the splash zone of a basin or even a lavatory.

There are many sealants on the market, some in squeeze-on application tubes, others in the form of a syringe. Most sealants come in a range of colours designed to match the standard colours of manufactured fixtures, but if you can't match the colour exactly, there are also clear sealants that dry to a transparent finish. You may want to apply a flexible sealant to large pieces of equipment such as the bath. Flexible sealants have some

'give', which is necessary in certain situations – for example, when someone gets into a bath, the combined weight of human and water may cause the tub to move a few millimetres. When the bather gets out and the water has flowed away, the bath may rise a little and return to

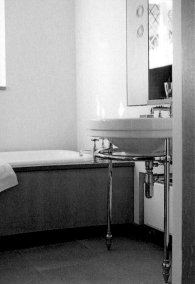

Above **Handbasins can be set into a surround similar to a kitchen worktop. They can be also be countersunk so that the upper surface is smooth and easy to clean. In a small bathroom this arrangement may provide useful storage space in built-in cupboards under and on either side of the basin.**
Left **Traditional basins, such as this one with an integral chrome towel rail, are often set on pedestals or stands.**

its previous position. This movement will weaken any rigid join between the bath and the wall. If the bath is made of cast iron or some other solid material, it may not be affected by such pressure, but the floor on which it is resting, especially if it is a wooden one, may sag a little under the weight and then rise again. The movement may be imperceptible, but over time a rigid sealer such as grout would start to crack and the gap between the bath and wall would gradually open up.

Many older homes have walls that are neither perfectly level nor straight. This can cause problems when tiling large areas because you may find that, if you start in the corner and work across the wall, building row upon row of tiles, your lines become less and less regular. It is a good idea to start in the centre of the wall and work out, following a plumb line rather than relying on the skirting board or the corners of the walls to guide you. When you reach the corners, small fillets of tile can be used to fill and finish – they are less obvious in a corner than in the middle of a room. You may also be concerned about fitting a shower cabinet or shower door to an enclosure against an uneven wall,

Below and right **Taps and spout can either be plumbed into the bath surround or wall-mounted, leaving the shape of the bath uninterrupted.** Far right **This classic plug is designed to fit neatly into the overflow outlet, which can be sited in the centre or at the end of the bath.**

but many manufacturers make doors that have generous rubber seals that are designed to accommodate a certain amount or irregularity.

Unless you are good at DIY, leave jobs such as putting up soap dishes, toothbrush holders, mirrors and towel rails to a professional – especially if the surface to which they are being attached is tiled or covered with a finish such as reinforced glass or marble. Drilling into tiles and other hard but brittle surfaces must be done with a diamond drill bit or similar to cope with the shiny or glazed finish and the hardness of the material. It may be tricky and time-consuming to repair a cracked or scratched tile.

Water softeners

Although they are not new, water softeners are less bulky that they used to be. Whether or not you need one depends on where you live and what your water is like. Hard water is a product of high levels of calcium and magnesium salts which are dissolved as rain water filters through rocks. The salts themselves are invisible in water but when heated they appear as limescale. Hard water is not harmful to your health, but if deposits of limescale build up in pipes and radiators, they can reduce the efficiency of the heating system and lead to increased running costs. You will also need more soap, shampoo and bubble bath to get a good lather if you live in a hard-water area.

A build-up of limescale in a shower head cuts down on its power and flow. Limescale deposits can also adversely affect enamel in a bath or shower tray and corrode the plating on taps. Hard water can even destroy new products. For example, a heated brass towel rail can suffer dezincification as soon as hard water starts to flow through it, and in extreme cases can rot within six weeks of installation. Water softeners can not only make the water you use in the bathroom pleasanter and easier on the skin – people suffering from eczema, for example, may find it gentler and less irritating – but they can also leave home-laundered clothes softer to the touch.

A water softener may also help to reduce the wear and tear on a range of equipment from lavatories to dishwashers and washing machines. Rather than installing small filter systems on each cold tap, it may be more

they have a similar effect to the electronic devices. Computerized scale inhibitors, again using electric current, send out a modulated audio frequency signal which transforms the electrical and physical properties of the scale-forming calcium nodules and prevents them from adhering to each other. There are also magnetic scale inhibitors on the market that operate in a similar fashion.

Below left **The shape of the spout and taps are important in respect of the overall scheme of the bathroom. A utilitarian, tubular spout works well with an angular basin, especially contemporary designs in steel, stone or glass.**
Below and right **The graceful curved or swan's neck style complements both classical and modern styles of basin and bathtub. The finish is important too. All the taps, spouts and waste outlets should match – whether they are in chrome, brass or nickel plate.**

economical to plumb a household-sized system into the main cold-water inlet. Softeners are operated by an ion exchange system: the hard water is passed through a resin, initiating a process whereby hard calcium and magnesium ions are replaced with sodium ions, which come from common salt. The salt solution on which the system depends usually needs to be topped up with salt on a regular basis. Some of these devices can lead to high levels of salt in the soft water, which makes it no good for drinking.

There are a number of electronic devices that 'condition' the water. They do not come into contact with the water itself, and do not therefore remove the hard salts, but they prevent them from forming a deposit. Radio waves are also used in some appliances –

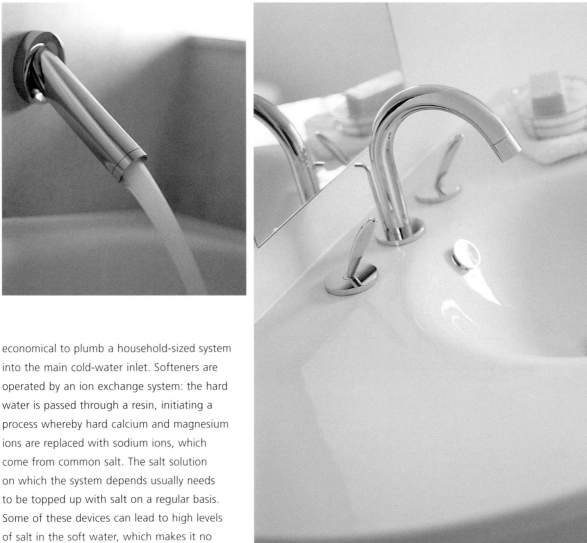

2
styles and spaces

indulgent

streamlined

small spaces

showers and wet rooms

FASHIONS IN BATHROOMS CHANGE SLOWLY. STYLES IN FIXTURES ARE NOT AS

SHORT-LIVED AS FASHIONS IN CLOTHES BECAUSE BATHS AND HANDBASINS ARE

CONSTRUCTED TO LAST MORE THAN A SINGLE SEASON, AND THEY ARE EXPENSIVE

TO REPLACE – INDEED, SOME THUNDERBOX LAVATORIES AND CAST-IRON BATHS

DATING FROM VICTORIAN TIMES ARE STILL IN REGULAR USE TODAY.

Since the 1950s, when bathrooms became a more widely integrated part of the house, there have been

various fashionable phases, often lasting a decade or more. The trends have been especially noticeable in

colours, but in general white has reigned supreme. With advances in technology and the introduction of

new materials, shapes have become more unusual and adventurous; at the same time the classic rolltop

bath has not only survived but it has become increasingly popular.

As the bathroom changed from being a place purely for washing to a haven linked with relaxation,

self-pampering, personal time and privacy, decoration became more important and indulgent. In the 1950s

and 1960s bathroom fixtures were predominantly pastel – blue, turquoise and primrose were among the

sought-after shades. In the 1970s colours grew darker, and acrylic baths, especially the luxurious corner

bath, were the latest thing. The colours then were chocolate brown, pampas and the ubiquitous avocado.

In the mid-1980s a vogue for everything white began to gather pace and bathroom styles became

retrospective rather than forward-gazing. Victorian and Edwardian designs were reproduced and allied

with modern plumbing technology, finishes and mass production, making them more widely available,

cost-effective and reliable. White fixtures offered an unrivalled basis for the creation of any mood or

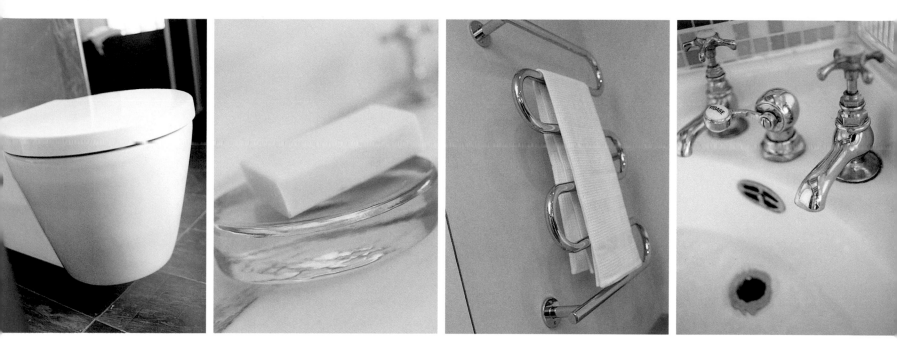

style. A bathroom with even the most daringly modern decoration is a suitable setting for a white rolltop bath, and a white lavatory can be paired harmoniously with colours as startling as vermilion and as pale as pink. White is also timeless – it does not date in the same way as a fashionably coloured suite.

In the 1990s designer names took on particular importance. Philippe Starck created his signature range for the Axor Hansgrohe group, and Dieter Sieger and Frank Huster brought the fashion for labels from the wardrobe and the sitting room into the bathroom. Other trends, such as the interest in Feng Shui and Zen, have made their mark on the bathroom. Japanese-inspired wooden tubs can now be found in minimalist settings and previously rare features such as Turkish-inspired steam rooms are now more commonplace.

New surface treatments have also provided a wider choice – ceramic tiles and vinyl wallpaper are no longer the only option. Concrete, once thought of as as cold and industrial, is tinted and finished to such a degree that it is not only acceptable but desirable indoors. Reinforced glass, now virtually unbreakable, is used for handbasins and baths as well as for large partitions and splashbacks.

The trend towards having more than one bathroom in a home offers great scope to the imagination, allowing you to decorate one, if not two, rooms in a scheme that is outrageous, indulgent or fun.

indulgent

An indulgent bathroom is a place to wallow in a bathful of scented foam or stand in a shower with torrents of steamy warm water cascading over you – a haven where you can indulge yourself physically and mentally. To satisfy these needs, the room should be spacious and comfortable with touches of luxury.

An indulgent bathroom can also be a place that allows you to gratify your decorating fantasies. Public rooms, such as sitting and dining rooms, may be in the best understated taste, and a bedroom shared with a partner a decorative compromise, but if you are lucky enough to have more than one bathroom, or a separate shower room, you have the opportunity to be really adventurous.

Vivid red and pink clashing tiles; a mural; an underwater theme – you can let your imagination roam free. An indulgent bathroom could also be the place to use an expensive paper or fabric – something that would be inordinately extravagant in a bigger room but is just affordable if you are buying no more than a single roll.

When planning an indulgent bathroom, make lists of colours you like, textures you enjoy, and images and themes – Indian, theatrical or woodland, for example – that you find attractive. Then tear out pages of magazines featuring ideas, accessories and rooms, and build up a reference file. You don't have to turn your bathroom into a replica or pastiche Indian temple; you can take elements of a pattern or a colour reference and use it in a subtle way that hints at the theme rather than

Right **A grandly proportioned bathroom is the only appropriate setting for this Victorian-style basin with pillar pedestal, raised sculpted back and wide surround.**
Centre **Placing a bath in the centre of the room makes it the dominant feature and dissects the main floor space. This extravagantly luxurious oval bath – with its wood-panelled casing, broad upper rim and plinth base – has been finished to resemble a piece of furniture.**

overstating it. The trend in this type of room is to take the best from the past and combine it with complementary examples of modern design. A classic rolltop bath fitted with a modern lever faucet reflects a successful blend of old and new, as does a modern bath with traditional crosshead taps. If you favour the mix-and-match approach, try to keep the fittings and shapes of the fixtures uniform. For example, select either chrome or brass taps and spouts rather than combining the two colours and types of finish, and for the bath, bidet, lavatory and handbasin choose shapes that are either rounded or angular, not both.

Comfort, convenience and luxury

The indulgent bathroom is a place to pamper your mind and body in serene and relaxing surroundings. Some people enjoy a long deep bath by candlelight with music playing and thick furry towels warming on a

Below left A double basin unit has been fitted under a graceful arch. The wall behind is mirrored, with the glass cut to accentuate the architectural shape, and slim mirror panels have been added at the sides. There is ample storage under the basins and in rows of small drawers beside the main cupboards.

Above Beaded lampshades on elaborate wall-mounted lights and a beaded fringe along the front edge of the basin complement an ornate mirror and a generously draped curtain. This is a decorative style that needs to be viewed and enjoyed at leisure; it is not for the purely functional bathroom.

heated rail ready to envelop them when they step out of the water. It may add to the pleasure to have comfortable objects in the room – a chair or chaise longue where the bather can lie and recover, wrapped in a deep-pile dressing gown, with a stack of magazines to read and maybe something to eat and drink.

An air of opulence can be achieved by adding a thick absorbent cotton mat over a parquet floor, pots of plants or flowers to provide colour and interest, and underfloor heating to ensure that even a mosaic tile or stone surface is comfortable to stand on and that no stepping-stone action from

allowing light into the room and giving a view of the sky in the upper half. Remember that, if a light is turned on inside the room, your outline will be silhouetted against the frosted glass – so for morning and evening bathing in winter you may need the additional shield of a blind or curtain.

An indulgent bathroom may also be reflected in the quality, style and type of its fixtures. A rolltop bath plumbed into the centre of a room gives an air of splendour because the bath is the focal point of the room and takes up more space than necessary. While retaining the classic shape and white-enamelled finish, the rolltop bath can be given elaborate finishing

Organic tactile surfaces such as wood, stone, plaster and glass can give a bathroom a human touch – an earthiness that is in strong contrast with the fast-moving, hi-tech world outside.

mat to mat is required to cross the floor. The arrangement of storage and shelves, soap trays and similar holders in the bathroom should be carefully thought out to enhance the sense of relaxation. It is enjoyable to be able to put out your hand and find a warm dry towel, the bottle of shampoo, a sponge, or whatever it may be, without having to get out of the bath and plod dripping across the floor. Having things to hand may extend to touch-sensitive remote-control panels that allow you to adjust the pressure of the jets in a spa bath or the temperature of the water with the mere touch of a fingertip. Automatic devices can be programmed to fill the bath or turn on the shower with water at a pre-set temperature.

When it comes to being indulgent, some people find that less is more and that serenity lies in simplicity and understated elegance. The eyes and mind can be soothed by the graphic lines and play of light on a glass basin or the view of the garden or treetops from the bathroom window. If you are an adherent of this philosophy, then the few items that you have in a bathroom can be of very good quality because you won't need to set aside money for additional decoration or accessories.

Light is an important factor in creating the right ambience. It is satisfying to be able to take a bath in daylight and stare out of the window without being seen. In many modern bathrooms such a sense of privacy can be achieved by installing a skylight or domed window in the roof. This enables the bather to contemplate clouds, treetops and birds in flight as though through a huge telescope, but without the danger of becoming a neighbourhood spectacle. If an overhead window is not feasible, you could put frosted glass into the lower half of a conventional wall-sited window. The opaque surface will preserve your modesty while

touches such as gilded claw feet or an interesting paint finish on the exposed sides. Reproduction Victorian- and Edwardian-style handbasins often have decorative finishes and integral features such as raised surrounds that wrap around the back of the basin and gradually taper down the sides, and soap recesses sculpted to resemble shells.

Large double-ended baths also need space. If the bath is for shared bathing, the plug and overflow should be located in the middle so that no one has to sit on the uncomfortable bit. Wall-mounted taps in the centre of the side of the bath also avoid the crick in the neck that can be inflicted by trying to keep the cold water spout out of your ear on one side and the hot one from burning your cheek on the other.

Corner baths, which were once thought the height of luxury, are now commonplace. They can be useful in an awkwardly shaped bathroom where the siting of the door and windows prevents the use of a single long wall to rest the bath against. Recent designs have favoured more angular shapes and can be based on a diamond rather than an oval inner recess. Some manufacturers include a seat area, which can be useful if you simply want to rinse your feet or give children somewhere to sit while they are being showered or washed. If showering is your preferred method of washing, you may choose an extra-large shower rose that

This sculptural bath has been designed with a stepped, curved wall to contain spray from the two showers – one on a flexible hose, the other on a rigid arm above the centre of the bath. Niches have been recessed into the corner to hold shower gels or bath preparations.

Far left The delicate wrought-iron and glass dressing table and chair provide the perfect place to apply cosmetics and style hair in this bathroom that doubles as a dressing room. The mirrors are placed so that they can be used while sitting or standing, and make use of the ample natural light.
Left Perfumes are best stored away from direct light since the sun can cause the scent to turn, and glass bottles are best kept out of the bathroom in case they fall against a hard surface and break.

gives a wider than average spray, a shower with an adjustable head that offers a range of spray types from needle-fine to massage, or a multi-jet shower cabinet where jets positioned at different heights give you an all-round wash.

Architectural details can add to the overall indulgent appearance of a bathroom. An archway or recess can be accented with colour or a mirror, or even used as a niche into which a shower or a handbasin and bidet can be plumbed. Door frames and skirting boards can also be highlighted with a different shade of paint from the walls.

You can also create architectural features. For example, you could construct a solid curved bench as part of the wall by the shower. The bench will in itself add a pleasing and interesting shape to the room but it may also be used to conceal pipes and provide a place to lay towels or clothes ready for when you emerge from the shower.

A window seat is another useful feature. The hinged top can be padded with a simple cushion and the boxed base provides storage space for bulky things such as toilet rolls or detergents and cleaning solutions.

Colours and materials

Colour is important in creating the right mood in a bathroom. As well as the natural palette of muted earthy colours such as cream, beige, soft greens and browns, which can have very relaxing and calming effects, there are other shades that may be used to create different moods in various lights. Yellow can be pale and

Far left Installing a bath and shower in separate areas of the same room gives plenty of space for both bathing and showering. Recessed up- and downlighters offer illumination that can be varied to suit the mood – either full-on for a brisk morning shower or more subdued for a leisurely soak. Efficient drainage is provided by a central grille set directly under the shower head.

Left Lining the edge of this bath with a mirrored surround is a simple way to make a small bathroom seem larger. It also helps to reflect light, making a dark or windowless room appear lighter.

refreshing in the morning daylight but warm and golden in subdued light or candlelight. A single wall of red can bring colour and interest to a room, being bright and vibrant in the daytime but rich and enveloping in artificial light – but be cautious about painting all the walls in a small bathroom with a strong red because the result may be overpowering and claustrophobic. Blue is a watery colour that can be refreshing first thing in the morning but in a dim light will contribute towards creating a restful and peaceful atmosphere.

Some people find that pattern in a bathroom can be distracting or overwhelming, but there are subtle ways of using it to add unobtrusive interest and a variation of colour. For example, different shades of mosaic tile can be used, tone on tone, to create the effect of a wash of colour across a room, or from the floor to the ceiling, getting gradually lighter towards the ceiling as though the observer were looking up at the sky from under the sea.

A couple of lines of contrasting colours of tile can create a mock dado effect and give definition to the space or delineate different areas in the room such as the shower, bath and handbasin. Classic patterns such as the geometric Greek key or Moorish crenellation will give a touch of exoticism without being overpowering.

Fabric is generally best kept to a minimum in a bathroom, but it may be used sparingly to add touches of colour and pattern. Decorative shower curtains can be made by lining a glamorous, untreated exterior fabric with a plain plastic shower curtain. For example, a length or off-cut of rich purple velvet could be lined with an off-the-peg shower curtain and hung over the bath. When someone is using the shower, the inner plastic curtain should be tucked inside the edge of the bath to contain splashes and the velvet left hanging over the outer edge so that the

Above and right Overflow outlets are plumbed through to the main waste pipe, which runs down the back of the basin and takes water from the main plug. Overflows are an important means of preventing flooding in both the basin and the bath. if the taps are left on by mistake, or if the bath is overfilled and runs over when the bather gets in, the overflow outlet can come to the rescue.

reverse side of the velvet is protected by the other curtain. This sort of two-layer curtain could also be used as a way of softening the angular lines of the bath and adding a touch of decadence.

Organic tactile surfaces such as wood, stone, plaster and glass give a human touch – an earthiness that is in strong contrast with the fast-moving, hi-tech world outside. Marble, limestone, granite and soapstone are good floor and surface materials because they are impervious to water and can be cut into relatively thin tiles and slabs so that the accumulated weight does not put a heavy burden on beams or boards.

Tongue-and-groove wooden boards can create an intimate atmosphere in a large room but may be overpowering and intrusive in a small room. Tongue-and-groove flooring can also create different moods: if it is

Top left **A floral design fired into the glaze makes this Victorian-style basin attractive as well as durable.**

Far left **The indulgent bathroom is the opposite of austere – an ornate candlestick or a fine old toy can be part of the decorative scheme.**

Left **Unusual fixtures such as this soap and jar holder may be found in antiques shops and markets and can be restored.**

Below left **Keep potions, lotions and cotton-wool balls in containers to avoid mess.**

Right **A rolltop bath takes pride of place in the period-style bathroom. The simple panelling, the figurative plaster roundel and the antique metal basin and stand add a few touches of luxury.**

painted in matt pale colours such as powder blue and stone, it can be reminiscent of the chic shoreline residences of New England around Nantucket and Cape Cod; in bright blue or red striped with white, it is more likely to give the impression of a Bognor or Brighton seaside theme; in subtle washes of green or lavender, the flooring may have Scandinavian overtones.

Concrete can be tinted and mixed with various resins to give a range of appearances, but ensure that the finish is smooth. Concrete with sharp peaks could graze your skin, and a roughly textured wall may trap moisture in small pockets, which may linger and become damp-smelling – and even encourage mould in a badly ventilated room.

Right and far right **Copper is a good conductor of heat – so a copper bath will warm through quickly, but it is wise to protect it with a seal. A copper bath must be well maintained to prevent residue water leading to a verdigris stain. This deep, Empire-style bath has centrally located taps and waste outlet so that the bather may choose at which end to recline.**

Various unusual materials have been used to create baths, among them glass, stone and copper. These are rare, usually custom-made, and therefore expensive, and they may require, on account of their weight, to be sited on a ground floor or one that has been specially reinforced. Copper and similar unenamelled metal baths require specialist cleaning, and wooden tubs, such as the Japanese-style bath that has become popular, are not suitable for use with detergents or certain soaps, whose cleaning and grease-cutting qualities will destroy the wood's natural oil. Some wooden baths also need to be kept constantly moist – otherwise the timber will dry out and shrink, and may split.

Spas and whirlpool baths

In a spa bath air is pumped into the tub through small jets arranged inside its base; when the bath is full, the jets of air send streams of bubbles rippling through the water. The bubbling effect creates a sparkling sensation on the

skin which is said to benefit blood circulation. Whirlpool baths generally work by recirculating the bath water, often through adjustable jets, allowing you to target particular areas of the body. They tend to have more powerful jets than a spa bath. A combination whirlpool and spa bath pumps a mixture of water and air into the tub. Designs at the top end of the range have a control that allows you to adjust the strength from a relaxing bath with a gentle ripple to a full-scale 'massage' treatment. Some types also have built-in heaters to prevent the water cooling while it is bubbling.

Many of the more expensive spa baths have built-in head and arm rests to support the bather comfortably. Underwater lighting, music systems and waterproof remote-control panels are also available for those who wish to pay for them. For pure indulgence there is the

Above **Although the black and white minimalist decoration could have given this bathroom a cold character, the warm wood flooring with black diamond inset – which complements the colour on the side of the rolltop bath – adds warmth and comfort. Glass shelves provide useful storage and display space, but because they are transparent they do not clutter up the wall.**

Far left **Mirror is a useful waterproof finish that can also be used as a facing to a cupboard or a bulky unit, where its effect will be to make the object less dominant.**

Left **Glass bricks are also bathroom-friendly and have the advantage of allowing light to pass through while partially obscuring the view. Their overall weight can be very heavy, so they need careful installation.**

Below right **Wood is another material that is suitable for a bathroom – or, as shown here, in a sauna – but ensure that the wood you choose is well seasoned and finished specifically for use in a bathroom.**

encouraging a good, deep sweat. The warmth of the steam is also said to increase blood flow and can be beneficial, but anyone with breathing difficulties, people with heart conditions and pregnant women should consult their doctor before entering a steam cabinet. You should also be careful about regulating the temperature of the steam, because steam stores and conducts heat more effectively than air and can rise to temperatures higher than those reached by boiling water.

All you need to make a steam room is a fully enclosed space such as a pod or capsule shower, or a purpose-built shower enclosure that is extended to the ceiling and has built in areas over the door and side panels. The steam generator, which resembles a big kettle, is kept outside the cabinet and can be plumbed in through a small opening in the wall or panel. The steam is pumped in through a nozzle until it gradually fills the space. Before installing a steam generator, check with the manufacturer of the shower cabinet or enclosure that the glass and rubber seals on the doors and supports are compatible with this sort of use.

Hydrosonic system by Teuco, which has whirlpool jets with ultrasound waves, which provide a deep muscle massage. This sort of treatment would be especially beneficial for people who feel stiff after long and frequent bursts of sport, gardening or golf, but for most of us the conventional spa or whirlpool is enough.

If you plan to have a spa or whirlpool system fitted to an existing bath, the installation should be done by a professional because it will require electrical wiring work, and adjustments may be necessary to suit the size and volume of your bath. With all spa and whirlpool baths it is advisable periodically to run a disinfectant through the system to prevent the build-up of bacteria and to give the interior pipework a thorough cleaning.

Before using bubble bath or other bath preparations in a whirlpool or spa system, check with the supplier that there is no danger that they could damage the pump mechanisms or reduce their effectiveness. You should also avoid using too much bubble bath because the aerating quality of such preparations can make the soapsuds overactive.

Saunas and steam rooms

Saunas are often sold as wooden cabinets, about the size of a small garden shed. Inside the cabinet are usually two rows of built-in benches or shelves to sit on – one at a lower, cooler level, the other at the higher, hotter position. Saunas encourage sweating and have a cleansing effect, but the atmosphere is drier than in a steam room, which can be awkward for people with breathing problems or for wearers of contact lenses.

Steam rooms are gradually taking over the luxury end of the market that was once dominated by jacuzzis and whirlpools. The steam room gives a wet heat, which is effective in cleansing the pores of the skin and

streamlined

The streamlined bathroom is primarily a place for quick washing and grooming. It is not, on the face of it, somewhere to linger. A bathroom of this type is defined by form and function; it is seen at its best first thing in the morning when the alarm clock sounds and you head straight for the shower, then over to the basin and back to the bedroom to get dressed. Everything in the room is designed to aid speed and efficiency.

The layout of the streamlined bathroom should be carefully planned, especially if two people are likely to be using the room at the same time. For example, it may make sense to arrange the fixtures and items of furniture in a linear fashion to allow enough space for one person to pass comfortably by the other. Before reaching any decisions, try to visualize the probable morning routine and walk through the scene in an imaginary bathroom to determine where the various objects should be positioned for maximum efficiency and ease of use.

Many manufacturers of ceramic and pressed steel bathroom suites have ranges with a contemporary edge that are styled to meet these requirements. Designers such as Dieter Sieger, Frank Huster and Philippe Starck have also brought their ideas and knowledge to bear on the development of a wider choice of products.

Computerized design and the availability of new materials have given manufacturers the ability to satisfy more specific needs. For example, there are shallow oblong basins that are perfect for cleaning teeth and washing hands. This type of basin does not require much water to fill and fits neatly into a narrow vanity unit or onto a bench-like unit – it may be all that is needed if you wash from head to toe in the shower and use an electric razor for shaving (if applicable). Shower cabinets also come in a wide variety of styles and finishes. Sculpted styles include a design made from overlapping curves, which has no doors to negotiate nor curtains to cling clammily to your warm wet skin. You simply walk in around the bend of the first curve, which is overlapped by the curve of the second, creating an enclosed pod. An alternative is a wet room – a waterproof showering area in which it doesn't matter where the spray flies.

The bath is usually a secondary element in this type of bathroom; but there are styles that have been designed to be linear rather than rounded, and where the inside is moulded in the shape of a figure of eight, so that the bath uses less water and provides a soak but within a more confined space than the oval corner bath or classic rolltop. The single-ended bath with a sloping incline at only one end is also suitable for a streamlined bathroom. As

Far left **More of a washing shelf than a basin, this fixture is long enough to allow two people to wash at the same time, but has been devised as a single length with a central drain. Its simple linear shape and functional form make it a strong feature in a streamlined bathroom.**
Left and below **Streamlined design does not mean that the space has to be cold, hard and unattractive.**

is the case with many contemporary kitchen features, the inspiration for the design of some of these bathroom fixtures springs from utilitarian settings such as hospitals.

Where the domestic kitchen has taken its style from the professional restaurant or hotel kitchen, the streamlined bathroom has drawn on features found in institutions such as prisons, factories and military barracks. These apparently unpromising sources use items of stainless-steel equipment that are functional, often minimally styled and simply finished – exactly the qualities that appeal to the designers of modern bathrooms.

The idea of a steel bathroom may seem cold and hard, but as long as the room is adequately heated there is no reason why it should be any colder or harder than cast iron or enamelled steel. Some steel baths are double skinned so that the air between the two layers acts as insulation against heat loss. The double thickness also gives the bath a more solid appearance than would otherwise be the case – the steel can be rolled in a slim

sheet that is perfectly viable but may appear rather thin and insubstantial. Steel baths often come in smooth sculpted shapes, and some manufacturers offer a choice between a highly polished 'mirror' surface and a more muted 'burnished' version. Their neat, uncluttered lines make steel bathroom fixtures easy to clean, but a non-abrasive cream or spray cleaner may be required to prevent scratching.

Traditional taps and spouts can complement modern fixtures but, if you are seeking speed and efficiency, some of the more recent innovations are worth considering. One of the more unobtrusive designs is Hansgrohe's combined overflow and bath tap in one minimalist fitting with a side lever to open the waste. Grohtec's Special Fittings range was originally designed for commercial use but is ideal for the hi-tech bathroom and can now be installed in domestic settings. The fixture is a single spout with an infrared electronic sensor; water flows – at a pre-determined temperature – only when the user's hands

Below left, below and right
In addition to well-designed storage space, the shower, handbasins and lavatory are generally more important than the bath in this style of bathroom. The functional elements may be grouped together, for ease of access, and the bath put at the far side of the room – becoming in effect a separate entity, to be used at another time. In this example, disc-shaped hot and cold knobs have been inserted into the bath surround, so that they remain within easy reach without interrupting the line of the broad oval rim.

are underneath the electronic sensing spot. Armitage Shanks's Sensorflow is another electronic system capable of detecting whether or not hands are present.

Lever taps are also appropriate in the streamlined bathroom. The single-lever mixer is a practical, elegant design that does away with the clutter of separate taps. The lever is simply moved from the cold to the hot end of the spectrum until the right temperature is established, and water flows through a single spout. Some lever taps come with a safety stop that controls access to the hot end of the lever's sweep, thereby preventing scalds.

If the streamlined bathroom is meant to be a relaxing venue, the lighting arrangement is important. The lights should be wired on two circuits, with dimmer switches, so that for the all-action morning routine the lights can be on full, targeting areas such as the handbasins and shower. In the evening, or at a quieter time of the day, the main over-basin lights can be dimmed or turned off, leaving a soft halo of light on the second circuit around

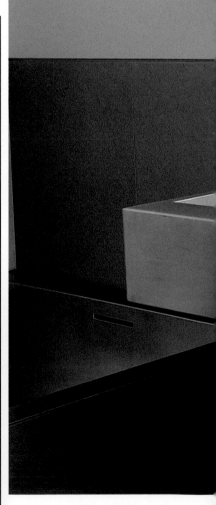

Right and far right **This single, custom-made metal basin is shallow compared with the traditional ceramic style, but the amount of water it holds is more than adequate for washing teeth, hands and faces. Specialist or cream cleaners should be used on this type of surface; those with an abrasive content may scratch or mark the metal.**

Above **The metallic theme is taken through to the lavatory, which is wall-hung with the tank concealed behind the wall.**

Left **A Philippe Starck mono basin mixer tap combines taps and spout in a single unit. The feather-like lever on top controls the flow and temperature of water. The lever is rounded and slightly curved, which makes it easy to hold and manoeuvre, even with wet hands.**
Below **This water spout is plumbed directly into the floor so that it arches neatly over the side of the bath.**

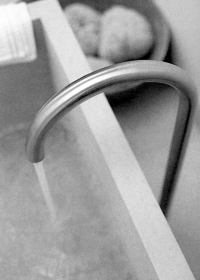

Top right **The tap is integral to the slim tubular support on which this glass basin is mounted. The flow and temperature of the water is selected by twisting the upper section of the pillar, which is a movable disc.**
Centre right **A plain spout is attached directly to the wall.**
Far right **Simple stylized levers instead of taps are used to supply hot and cold water to a mixer spout.**

the periphery of the room. Another option is to direct a couple of dimmed lights onto the bath and extinguish the other circuit, leaving the rest of the room in darkness. Burning incense or joss sticks will add a subtle scent to the air, and candles and deep-pile towels can also be put to good use.

Mirrors are another important element of the streamlined bathroom. The mirror behind the handbasin must be not only functional but also aesthetically pleasing. There is no point in having a badly illuminated, small mirror that requires you to stretch over the basin and allows you to glimpse only a small part of yourself at one time. One option is to mirror the whole area behind the handbasin or basins. This can be done with a single large sheet of mirror or a grid of mirror tiles.

The mirror's glass facing is waterproof and will serve as an easy-to-clean splashback as well as providing an ample viewing area. If you

choose this option, put a generous line of sealant or some other filling device between the mirror and the basin or any supporting unit; otherwise water may seep behind the mirror and damage the silvered backing. In a steamy bathroom, water will condense when it comes into contact with the coolness of the mirror and the drops of water will trickle down the surface and seep through cracks or joins at its base.

If you prefer a mirror for individual use, consider the classic Eileen Gray design that has a small mirror on an adjustable arm in front of the large one. Modern copies of this are available, and the small mirror is usually a magnifier, which is perfect for close scrutiny. Double-sided magnifying mirrors are widely available on extendable metal arms that can be pulled forwards and pressed back flat to the wall surface as required. This type of mirror is useful for shaving, applying make-up or inserting contact lenses.

A casual display or arrangement of some natural objects can prevent a streamlined room from looking too clinical. For example, a glass or stone bowl or a simple basket filled with natural sponges, a couple of loofahs and a Japanese lather brush would create an effect that is both decorative and appropriate to the setting. If you are concerned to keep cleaning simple, avoid dust-gathering items such as bowls of potpourri, sample soaps and miniature shampoo bottles from hotels and frilly, floral-printed fabric covers for tissue boxes and toilet rolls.

If a streamlined bathroom opens directly into another room, such as a bedroom or dressing room, you may wish to disguise the fixtures to give the impression that the bathroom is a continuation of the other room. One way to do this is to create a wall or doors behind which a

Above By varying the levels in a room you can create the illusion of spaciousness. This en suite bathroom has steps leading up to a raised level from which the sunken bath can be reached.
Above right and right **The bidet and lavatory have been hung onto the side of the bath – a practical arrangement that means that all the wastepipes can be ducted away from the same area and concealed behind a single façade. The shower is located behind a simple reinforced glass panel. Folding doors between the bedroom and bathroom can be closed over to create privacy in either area – or opened out to provide a generous vista.**

Right **Cupboard space below a basin is useful because it allows you to keep the toiletries you need close to hand and put them away easily when they are no longer required. This cone-shaped unit has been fashioned in a modern style from a traditional material.**

shower and a handbasin, for example, are hidden. In such situations the cupboards that house the fixtures should be fitted with extractor fans to expel moisture and steam. Some options for creating streamlined bathrooms in small spaces are examined in the next section, pages 68–79.

Colours and materials

Although the streamlined bathroom is often conceived as an unfussy, somewhat austere area, you can introduce elements of modern glamour that harmonize with its practical character. White is a favourite colour for this room because it gives a fresh, clean, simple appearance, but be careful to ensure that the bathroom does not take on a cold and institutional appearance. Touches of colour can soften the strictness and make the place warmer and more inviting, but try to restrict the scheme you use to one main colour and a contrasting one or to two or three shades of the same colour.

A soft wash of an earthy tone, such as a hint of green or beige, will reduce the austerity of a predominantly white room. If there are plenty of steel or chrome surfaces in the room, you may discover that paints and fabrics with blue or turquoise overtones only enhance the impression of coolness, but if the blue is mixed with a little pink, creating a shade that is closer to lavender, then a warmer effect will be achieved.

Acid colours such as citrus yellow and fluorescent lime can be effective with white and steel and give a bright, zesty edge to a scheme. Strong and fashionable colours of this type should be used sparingly and preferably as a paint or in an accessory so that when the trend passes, or you tire of the colour, it can be removed easily. If you use such a colour in tiles or another more permanent feature, it will be messy, expensive and time-consuming to replace.

Window treatments can be used to add colour and interest. Roller blinds made with a finely punched or perforated random design will allow light to filter through and create patterns on the walls and floors. A tone-on-tone striped fabric can also be used as a blind and will provide pattern and a variety of shades of a single colour. Fine-slat louvre blinds come in a wide range of colours and unusual finishes, including metallic, and have a businesslike appearance.

The floor surface in a streamlined bathroom should be waterproof and easy to wipe down; underfloor heating could do away with the need for slippers, making it an

even simpler place to walk into and use. If the room has minimal decoration, the floor may be a place to introduce a little colour, texture or pattern. There are many modern floor tiles that have specks of reflective material in them, giving the impression that they contain a sprinkling of gold, silver or titanium.

One flooring option for this type of bathroom is textured rubber – another idea that has its roots in industrial warehouses and hospitals. Rubber flooring is hardwearing and has a warmer feel underfoot than unheated stone and ceramic surfaces; it can also provide a certain level of heat and sound insulation.

Some people prefer a good-quality, vinyl-tile copy of marble, granite or slate flooring to the real thing because the imitation is warmer, softer and, in most cases,

cheaper. Fake wooden floors with finishes ranging from parquet to 'driftwood' are also worth considering for a heavily used bathroom because they have the appearance of wood but can be easily wiped clean of splashes without the fear of marking or staining that comes with a genuine wooden floor.

On shiny floor surfaces such as marble or polished ceramic tiles take care to use non-slip bathmats. A bathroom is full of hard surfaces, and to slip and fall against one could be painful. Many bathmats are sold with a light rubber mesh on the back which grips the floor surface, or you can buy a double-sided grip backing that can be attached to the mat and the floor, but as bathmats need regular machine-washing it is advisable to buy one that has an integral back.

Cork and wooden mats are a good alternative to a cotton or fabric mat, although you need to be sure that the cork has been sealed – or it will absorb water and gradually disintegrate. Wooden mats or duckboards are made from lengths of wood secured over a frame, rather like decking found in gardens. These boards allow the water to drip from you onto the floor rather than absorbing the moisture, so they should be used only on waterproof flooring.

Surfaces and storage

To maintain the integrity of the streamlined look, endeavour to keep surfaces uncluttered. A cupboard directly beside the sink, with a door opening away from you, provides easily accessible storage for most of the items that commonly accumulate around the basin or on the shelf above it.

The surfaces in a bathroom look best when they are clean. Products such as toothpaste and shaving gel tend to leave opaque marks and residues, and hairs may accumulate on the shelf in front of the mirror and in the plughole, so for easy cleaning it is advisable to keep the basin, bath and shower areas free of bottles and cosmetic products. The more laborious option is to pick up the bottles and tubes, move them, do the cleaning, and then replace them.

Many beauty preparations and products based on liquid soap are greasy and prone to leaking, so you may choose to line the shelves on which they are stored with an easily removable rubber mat that can be taken out and showered clean. Reinforced-glass shelves and ceramic tiles

Above **The moulded basin and surround eliminates all the joins and cracks that can harbour germs or bits of fluff and grime. This basin will need to be wiped often, and even polished, to avoid marks from toothpaste and soap scum.**

Top right **Decant bath and shampoo products into sturdy, unbreakable metal or plastic containers.**

Below right **A functional hook for towels or robes.**

are equally easy to clean with a damp cloth. Some people use a narrow towelling mat, a small hand towel or a couple of face cloths as shelf liners. The towelling absorbs the drips and moisture that may have covered the bottles in the shower or during use. When the mat becomes stained or marked, it can easily be taken away, washed and replaced with another.

To keep the number of bottles and jars in your bathroom to a minimum, be disciplined about finishing off one bottle before opening another. If you stop using a product or find that one doesn't suit you, throw it out there and then. Don't store things at the back of a shelf or cupboard thinking that they will come in useful some time – almost invariably they simply gather dust until you move house or redecorate the room. In addition to the regularly used products that need to be within easy reach, spare items can also be kept in the bathroom, if there is enough space. Then, if you run out of something while having a bath, it will save you having to get dry, find a dressing gown and go looking for them elsewhere in your home. Ideally there should be storage space for spare lavatory paper, cotton wool,

with the products recommended by the manufacturer. As well as being a place for bathing, the bathroom is often where you undress so it is a sensible place to have a laundry bag, sack or basket. For a bachelor pad, a calico or linen bag hanging on a peg behind a door may be enough, but for a household of two or more people a larger receptacle will be required. In a streamlined bathroom the container could be a slick chrome

Equipment found in prisons, factories and military barracks is functional, often minimally styled and simply finished – exactly the qualities that appeal to modern bathroom designers.

tissues, toothpaste, soap, shampoo and shower gels. Another type of storage to consider in a streamlined bathroom is hanging space for dressing gowns, towels in use and clothes that have been taken off or are waiting to be put on. Towels should be hung on a rail to dry; if left damp and screwed up, they may become musty-smelling. A chair, window seat or the top of a laundry basket are frequently used to lay clothes on, but an interesting alternative is the Shaker peg rail, which – though neither hi-tech nor a modern piece of design – provides an eminently efficient hanging system.

A Shaker peg rail, or a modern interpretation with metal hooks or horn-shaped pegs, can be screwed along the wall above head height so that it does not impede movement or cause things to catch on it. The back board can be painted to match the wall so that it almost disappears – or, if you want to make a feature of it, paint it in a contrasting shade. The pegs may be used for hanging up all sorts of things such as clothes and towels, but in the streamlined bathroom this should be done with restraint – otherwise the peg rail could come to resemble an untidy washing line.

Open shelving can be an attractive feature in a bathroom but in this style of room the items that are on display should be uniform or of similar colours and shapes. They should also be able to tolerate a damp and steamy atmosphere. A pile of neatly folded towels in a single colour is useful as well as attractive – as the towels will be used, washed and replaced, there is no need to worry about their becoming damp or mouldy, or collecting dust.

Glass shelves are inconspicuous and light, easy to clean and timeless but, for safety, they must be laminated or made of a reinforced material. Perspex has a similar barely visible appearance to glass and is safer because it is virtually unbreakable, but it can become cloudy from numerous little scratches on the surface and should be cleaned only

pedal bin, perhaps lined with a removable and washable cloth inner bag that can be easily lifted out when full and transported to the washing machine. Wicker baskets have long been popular, especially the style known as the Ali Baba, but the outer edges of the wicker may be rough and can snag tights and other fine materials.

Opaque, lightweight plastic bins in interesting colours are also available – they have the advantage of being easily cleaned and dried should any wet clothes be dropped inside them or water splashed on the outside when someone is using the bathroom.

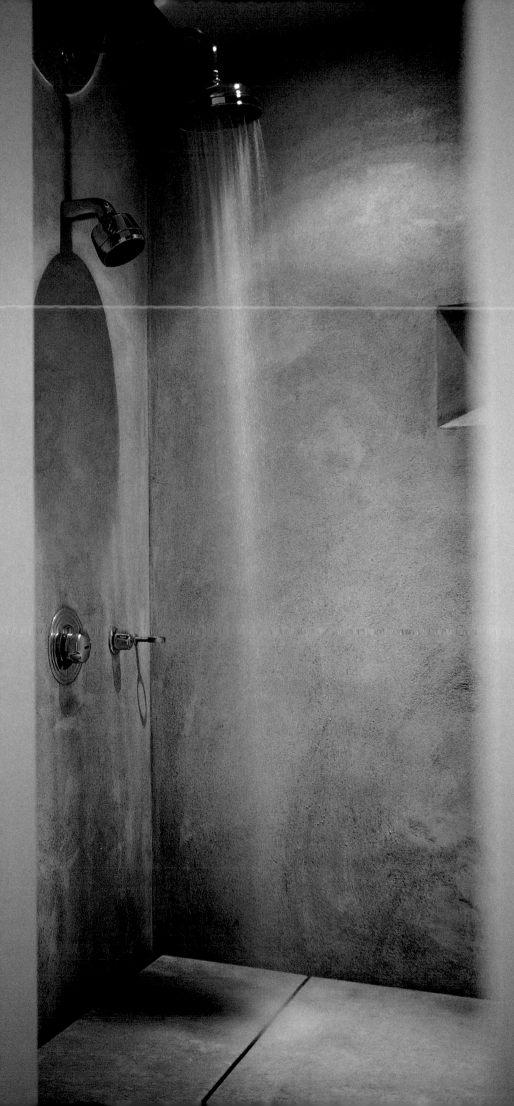

small spaces

A combination of improved plumbing, better and smaller pumps and specially designed fixtures means that smaller and smaller areas, including niches once dismissed as 'dead spaces', are now being utilized to make bathrooms. The broom cupboard, the all-important glory hole under the stairs where stacks of old magazines lurk, is just the sort of place that is increasingly likely to be transformed into a shower, bath or cloakroom.

A brief inspection of the broom cupboard would probably leave you with the impression that there is no way in which a useful washing facility could be installed in such a small space – there would be hardly enough room to stretch out a towel and dry yourself, let alone to accommodate bulky bathroom equipment. But you may be surprised to discover how, with careful planning and the selection of well-designed fixtures, it is possible to create a viable cloakroom or bathroom in the most apparently unpromising places.

To assemble some ideas, consider and study other small spaces containing washing facilities. For example, many hotel bathrooms are compact but luxurious. A yacht's 'head' is likely to have a small countersunk basin with a lid that can be closed over it to make a useful surface, as well as a shower installed over a removable section of wooden flooring that hides a shower tray. In aircraft, the necessary facilities are crammed into a tiny space – but they nevertheless serve the purpose they were designed for, even when in almost constant use thousands of metres up in the sky.

Different types of use

When you have found your space, you must decide what exactly you require – a small main bathroom, en suite or otherwise, an ancillary bathroom or a cloakroom.

Even if there is no overriding need for a second washing facility in your home, using a small space to add a second bathroom can bring bonuses. For example, guests who stay overnight or for a weekend will enjoy having their own bathroom. It will make them less self-conscious about emptying out the contents of their washbags and leaving them lying around, and when they

Opposite page **A linear arrangement of fixtures often makes the best use of space in a narrow bathroom. Here the bath is placed at the far end of the room. At its foot is one of a pair of basins mounted on a simple stone base, and beside it stands a shower with clear glass walls, which contain the spray without restricting** the view. On the near side of the shower are a lavatory and the second basin. The passageway of narrow-slat wooden decking provides a slip-proof floor covering that is also warm under bare feet.

Left and below **The wall beside this bath is glass, which can be left unlit and transparent with a view through to the bedroom,** making the space seem larger and allowing extra light to shine through. The glazed panel incorporates an interlay that becomes opaque at the flick of an electrical switch, giving privacy to anyone using the bathroom. Because the edge of the bath can be seen from the bedroom, it is kept clear of bottles and soap.

wake up in the morning they will not feel under pressure to spend as little time as possible in the bathroom while a queue builds up outside. Installing a second bathroom may also increase the value of your home and, when you come to sell, could give your property an edge over similar properties on the market.

The small main bathroom found in a modern flat or studio apartment in a converted building is often the only enclosed space and may be located in a space that was never intended to be a bathroom. Its position may have been dictated by the way in which the house or block was divided into apartments – to give easy access to pipework or for some other practical rather than aesthetic reason.

But, as the saying goes, small can be beautiful. Whatever your 'raw material', it is well worth spending time on the research and planning for this type of room. A sheet of graph paper marked out with the dimensions of the space and squares of paper cut out to the size and shape of the fixtures are very useful tools if you want to examine the various options. Move the larger pieces around until you find areas where there is enough wall space to support them, then try to squeeze in the ancillary equipment around them.

Below **An uncomplicated, cabinet-like shower enclosure and a narrow, double trough sink provide adequate facilities for washing and occupy a minimal amount of space.**

Left and top **This bathroom follows a linear design. The bath has been fitted into an area with restricted head room – which is acceptable because the bath is intended purely for sitting or lying in. The shower, lined with small mosaic tiles, has been plumbed in at the other end of the room, where the walls reach above full head height.**

Above **A shower has been fitted in behind the basin by using a gently curving wall and a basin specifically designed to fit into a corner. Glass bricks allow a good flow of natural light into both the shower and the bathroom. The blue mosaic tiles add to the impression of light and freshness, which is important in a small space.**

A secondary bathroom is often installed to relieve demand on the main bathroom. When planning such a room, you need to determine its main function. Will it be at its busiest when the children are getting ready for school? Do they prefer having baths or showers? If you simply need a back-up bathroom for quick washing, don't try to squeeze in a bath – simply plumb in a shower and make more practical use of the remaining space.

If the small second bathroom is intended to be a place where you can lock yourself away in a soapy tub for relaxation while the main bathroom bears the brunt of the family wear and tear, then you could choose a bath with a hand-held shower as part of the tap fitment, or perhaps an over-bath shower with a curtain rather than a solid panel.

Depending on the dimensions of the room and what facilities are available elsewhere in your home, you will also have to make decisions about what equipment is required in addition to the shower or bath. For example, it is always useful to have a lavatory adjacent to the bath or shower, so that you once undressed you do not have to put your clothes back on to go to another room.

People seeking the luxury of en suite bathrooms are often persuaded to install them in small spaces. While they may be keen to have washing facilities in an integral or adjacent space, they are unwilling to lose valuable floor area in the bedroom. Architectural features such as archways or recesses on either side of a fireplace can lend themselves to being incorporated in a scheme of this kind, and extra space may also be found by moving a doorway or incorporating into the bathroom a section of the end of a corridor or passageway.

Ventilation and storage

Some people like to conceal an en suite shower or lavatory in a cupboard or built-in wardrobe so that it does not encroach upon the rest of the room. Ventilation is especially important in such circumstances because of the need to ensure that the cupboard or other enclosure does not become damp or humid. If you plan to include a shower in this kind of room, consider a sealed unit, with built-in roof and tray, that will contain much of the steam and water within its walls.

The relative lack of air in a small room means that odours tend to linger there longer than they would in a larger room. To counteract this, it is advisable to fit an

Above **A wall-mounted basin saves precious millimetres in a small bathroom. If the basin were built into a unit, it would appear more solid and boxy, making the space around it seem smaller. The curved, wall-mounted towel** rail **is also an economical way of heating the room and drying towels without taking up floor area.**
Right **In a room that is well waterproofed – such as this one, which is completely tiled – a shower door or** curtain **may be unnecessary, and an open shower will make the room appear larger. In addition to the overhead shower there are nozzles plumbed into the wall so that water will spray out at various levels.**

efficient ventilator and to keep an air freshener or similar perfume-based product close to hand. One option is a fan that turns itself on automatically when a light switch is pressed or which can be triggered by a device in the door that activates the fan when the door is opened.

Although storage space is frequently at a premium in these small rooms, you should ideally avoid putting up too many cupboards or wall-mounted accessories because

Brighten a windowless room by placing a small window frame in front of a piece of opaque glass and setting a small light behind the glass to give the impression of daylight beyond.

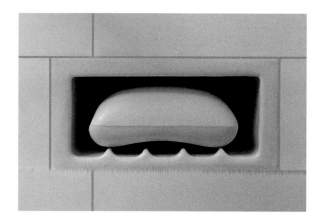

This 1930s-style bathroom has a ceramic bath with a rounded edge and the walls have been tiled with period-style brick-shaped ceramics. Instead of a rigid shower panel, water-repellent curtains have been hung to complement the rounded shapes of the suite. They can be drawn back and decoratively draped when the bath alone is being used.

these will make the walls appear to be closing in and give the impression that the room is even smaller than it is. Keep cupboards and other storage facilities up high, above eye level and preferably above head level, so that they are not immediately apparent when you walk into the room. You could build a single narrow shelf around the perimeter of the room so that narrow or smaller objects can be stored there – but, for safety's sake, do not position it over the bath, in case things fall off. As long as the items are neatly stored, preferably in opaque watertight plastic boxes, they will not dominate the room.

If you decide to use plastic boxes for storage, make sure that they are of a uniform design or colour rather than a jumbled collection, and reserve each box for no more than one type of item – medicines, make-up or bath potions, for example. Keep the ones you use most frequently close to hand. Those containing rarely used items – such as mosquito repellent that is required only during holiday periods, or false eyelashes for wearing at parties – can be stored in less accessible places.

Creating an illusion of spaciousness

The decoration of a small room can either add to the feeling of space or detract from it – at worst, the room may be reminiscent of a dark damp cave.

There are several things that you can do to make a small space seem larger. Choosing light colours and plenty of white will brighten up a dark or windowless room. Dark colours can evoke a cosy intimate feeling, but they should be used sparingly – otherwise the effect may be claustrophobic. If you are passionate about rich dark colours, try using one such colour on a single wall and a much paler tone of the same colour on the other walls – or use the dark colour on the woodwork and the lighter shade on the walls.

Mirrors are a great way of creating an illusion of space, but don't overdo them in a small room – it can be disorientating to be greeted first thing in the morning by a vision of yourself infinitely reflected. If there are no windows in the room, you can introduce a window-style feature by putting a mirror behind a small window frame, or by placing the frame in front of a piece of opaque glass and setting a small light behind it to give the impression of daylight beyond.

Flooring and lighting can also be used to enhance a feeling of spaciousness. For example, if you have a wooden-plank floor, you could lay the length of the plank parallel with the longest wall, or towards the door, so that the eye is drawn along the length of the plank. If there is a striped or linear pattern in a linoleum or a vinyl tile, lay it in the same way.

If a small bathroom or cloakroom has a central ceiling light, the eye is drawn to the level of the illumination, making the ceiling appear lower, whereas a row of recessed spots will be neat and flush with the ceiling, giving a more spacious feel.

Useful equipment

Equipment that has been specially designed for small bathrooms includes the Sitz bath, which has been popular for a long time on the European continent. This is a deep square tub with an integral seat. When someone is immersed in a Sitz bath, the water level reaches the height of the upper chest.

There are also many modern baths specifically designed to be suitable for small rooms. These tend to be shorter than the more luxurious styles, and some of them taper to

follow the shape of the body; this means that the head end is wide enough to accommodate the width of shoulders and hips, but the bath then curves inwards to follow the line of the legs and feet. Saving space in this way may enable you to put a handbasin at the foot end without having to sacrifice the pleasure of a real bath. These tapering baths are usually available in right- and left-handed versions so that they can be used on either side of a room.

If you wash your hair in the bath or shower and feel that a large handbasin is a waste of space, then choose one of the many small ones on the market. These include industrial ones that slot into the wall in an upright fashion leaving a small recess in the bottom to catch the water. The taps can be plumbed in at the side of the basin rather than in the centre at the back, which also saves space.

There are a number of corner basins on the market that have been specifically designed to fit into the right angle where two walls meet. These can be useful for installing behind doors or in areas where flat wall space is scarce. The typical basin has a triangular integral ceramic corner that fits between the two walls and the bowl sits in front. This kind of basin can be held up securely on brackets screwed into the walls and does not need a pedestal support.

A towel rail that has been inserted under the front edge of the sink not only provides an appropriate place to hang a hand towel but also, when the towel is in place, offers a means to conceal the unsightly wastepipe under the basin.

The fact that it is much easier than it used to be to keep pipes hidden is a boon in a small bathroom. Rather than the place being dominated by ugly brackets and long stretches of pipe, most of this functional spaghetti can now be disguised or eliminated. Enclosing the lavatory cistern behind a half-height false wall, for example, reduces the amount of ceramic on show, and the top of the cover, which should be hinged to give access to the top of the cistern, can double as a shelf. It also means that the cistern can be a cheap plastic one rather than a more expensive ceramic design.

Wall-hung lavatories and handbasins are also worth considering for a small bathroom or cloakroom because the absence of pedestals conveys the appearance of more floor space. If you decide to install such fixtures, allow for a slight overlap when measuring up, so that the edge of the basin can occupy a small part of the area above the lavatory bowl – those valuable millimetres can make a difference.

Another feature that may need to be introduced into a small bathroom – especially if it the only enclosed space in an open-plan apartment – is a retractable washing line. If a washing line is positioned over the bath, it can be useful for drying lingerie as well as the hand-washed woollens that have a tendency to drip for some time, and it can be wound back into its case when not in use.

The pros and cons of showers

It is not particularly likely that you will have space to accommodate a separate shower in a small bathroom unless you are prepared to live without a bath altogether. Many people like to have the option of either bathing or showering and, even though your personal preference may be for a shower, think about showing off the apartment to a potential purchaser when you come to move on; offering both a bath and a shower will be a strong selling point, especially if it is your only bathroom.

The most efficient way to incorporate a shower into a confined space is to install it over the bath so that the bath itself doubles as a shower tray.

When it comes to containing the spray from a shower over the bath, there are three alternatives. Your choice will depend on your budget and your personal bathing preferences. The cheapest and simplest option is a shower curtain hung from a pole. The main disadvantage of this arrangement is that a cold plastic shower curtain clinging to your bare skin can be a severe distraction from the pleasures of bathing. Also, you may need to search hard to find a style of curtain that harmonizes with the rest of your bathroom decor.

A more sophisticated course of action would be to erect either a screen made of reinforced glass along part of the side of the bath or sliding glass panels that enclose one whole side of the bath. All these options are examined in more detail on pages 80-91, in the section devoted to showers and wet rooms.

Cloakrooms

A cloakroom is useful not only as a place for hanging coats (if there is space) but also as a means of dispersing the load on the main bathroom. In a home constructed on more than one level, a cloakroom on a different floor from the main bathroom is an arrangement that benefits everybody – particularly toddlers and elderly people, who may not have to walk as far as they otherwise would have done to reach a lavatory. A cloakroom is often just big enough to accommodate a lavatory and handbasin; there is generally no room for bath or shower.

In some situations it may seem as though there is barely enough space for the basics – but, if you are convinced that a cloakroom would bring benefits to the general running of your home, it is worth trying to overcome the hurdles. There are a number of fixtures on the market that may give you the means to transform what appears to be an impossibility into a reality.

For example, a leading British manufacturer now produces a lavatory seat with a sideways orientation that enables you to sit comfortably at an angle, thereby avoiding physical contact with the handbasin, and perhaps escaping a burn from the radiator. If your household is predominantly male, a urinal could be the solution – a wall-mounted one would take up less space than an ordinary lavatory. There is even news from Scandinavia of the development of a female urinal, but such a fixture is not yet on the market.

Some of the options for handbasins in small bathrooms have been discussed earlier in the chapter. It is important in a cloakroom, more than anywhere else, to keep the clutter on a basin to a minimum – opt for a single bar of soap or a liquid soap dispenser and try to avoid bulky soap dishes and decorative but unnecessary items such as baskets of potpourri.

In a cloakroom, as in a small bathroom, it is not advisable to box things in or to install a cupboard under the basin because the resulting structures will take up valuable space. If you really need some form of storage under the basin, a couple of narrow graduated shelves – a wider and longer one at the top, and a narrow, short one at the bottom – will help. The shelves can be concealed behind a canvas or plain fabric curtain that will act as a screen but do no damage if someone sitting on the lavatory knocks their knees against it.

Storage cupboards are best installed above the height of the basin, but position them carefully so that people using the cloakroom are not in danger of cracking their heads or poking their eyes on the corners.

The back of the door to the cloakroom is a space whose usefulness is often overlooked. The door can be an excellent site for a mirror and towel ring and, if it is within easy reach, even a lavatory roll-holder.

Below **This silver and black paper has a shiny reflective surface, which can brighten up a windowless cloakroom.** Below right **Mirror is a useful material for a splashback.** Right **This basin and shower enclosure has a glass wall whose middle section has been frosted – not only enhancing the decorative scheme but also making it more conspicuous. It is unlkely that anyone would walk into a frosted pane – which might happen if the whole wall were clear glass. The opaque band is at the right height to provide a certain amount of modesty screening for a naked adult.**

showers and wet rooms

Showers are exhilarating and refreshing. It is believed in the Orient that the fast-flowing water falling over your body enhances Ch'i, or positive energy. As well as boosting your vitality, showers cleanse, washing away dead skin and sweat which, if you have a bath, tends to stay in the water with you. In Japan it is common to shower first to cleanse the body, then to sit in a tub of warm water to soak and relax.

Many people find that taking a shower is an ideal way to start the day – a blast of water from head to foot, washing away sleepiness and preparing the mind and body for the day. There are also situations in which a shower is more appropriate than a bath. For example, a shower after sport is a marvellous way to cool down and wash away perspiration, and people with mobility difficulties can find it easier to walk into a shower enclosure and sit down than to get up and down in a bath.

Showering tends to be a less time-consuming exercise than having a bath. It is also more ecologically sound because it uses considerably less water – a single bath is reckoned to use the same amount of water as five average-length showers.

If you are planning to install a shower, you need to know what power (usually calibrated in bars) is necessary to obtain a strong flow of water and whether or not a pump is required. There is often confusion about what is really wanted in a shower. Some people think that the water spray should be strong enough to blast them from one side of the enclosure to the other – but what they really need is a good-sized shower head that yields an adequate amount of spray. As important as the size of the shower head is an efficient supply of water. Aerated water – which is simply water mixed with air – gives the effect of a strong shower but uses less water than a conventional system.

As a general rule, for a shower to function satisfactorily without a pump, the distance between the base of your main water tank and the head of your shower should be at least 4 metres. If you don't have a tank and your water comes directly from the mains and is heated by a combination or instantaneous boiler, it will probably be impossible to fit a pump.

An electric shower may be the answer. The standard electric shower is connected to the cold-water mains supply and the water is heated as it passes through the unit. You only heat the water as you use it so there is no waste. There are also mixer showers that draw hot and cold water from the main household supplies. Both the electric and mixer showers can be bought with built-in pumps which boost the water-flow rate. There

often recessed into the ceiling, must be specifically designed for this type of use. Standard fittings are not sealed and may be dangerous if they come into contact with moisture.

Another idea is to build the walls of the enclosure from glass blocks, which not only let light through but also have good insulation properties. The blocks are available as clear glass or in colours such as green, turquoise, royal blue and gold – you can use a single colour throughout or a mosaic mix of all. Good-quality glass blocks come with a PVC collar which has interlocking grooves to ensure that the blocks fit tightly on top of each other before they are fixed with a special adhesive.

The third option is the freestanding cubicle. The cubicle has a shower tray, walls and roof in one moulded pod which can be put virtually anywhere because it does not need to be against a wall. This type of unit is appropriate in an en suite bathroom or where a shower is needed

quickly. It is pre-fabricated and may be easily installed, and there is no assembly, tiling, grouting or sealing to be done. Basic units come in a standard design and a range of pastel colours in addition to white. The modules tend to be practical but not very stylish, with a choice of doors that includes corner-entry, pivot or bi-fold. Space inside is fairly limited, and some cabinets come with an opaque or clear roof to admit light and relieve the sense of being shut in.

At the other end of the spectrum are spacious freestanding cubicles that come with built-in steam-sauna function, electric lights and aromatic herb dispenser. They may also have an integrally moulded seat and a programmable electronic up-and-down device that allows you to place the water jets where you want them. Some have thermostatic mixers so that you can have a shower at your preferred, pre-set temperature. Foot, back and vertical massage jets may also be an option.

The pod or freestanding cubicle has an integral shower tray, but in the purpose-built shower cabinet you could seal and tile the floor as well as the walls, creating a miniature wet room. In most cases, however, your preferred option will probably be to build in the largest available pre-cast enamelled or acrylic tray. While building in the rim on either side of the tray, the surround can be extended upwards to create a shelf or, if there is room, a seat.

Shower trays come in various shapes and sizes. The standard ones are square but corner shapes and oblongs are also available and there are some with circular recesses within a square frame. Trays are made in a variety of materials including cast iron, steel, composite and enamelled fireclay. More recently, as part of the trend for more natural and organic materials, stone has been gaining in popularity.

Unpolished stone has the advantage of having its own non-slip surface, but in the case of the enamelled and other shiny-surface trays it is important to have a non-slip finish. Most manufacturers create a raised pattern within the tray, the ridges of which provide a non-slip grip; alternatively you can add a rubber mat, strips of self-adhesive textured banding or a wooden duckboard.

The problem with many of the textured adhesive strips is that they can, in time, become stained and grubby-looking, and they are difficult to clean. It can be easier to replace them than to try to remove the grime. There is no standard height for a shower head other than its distance

Far left **The shower enclosure is an integral part of this bathroom. A large recess has been created by building an enclosing third wall, but the fourth side has been left open to the rest of the room.**
Left **Slim shelves of reinforced glass provide water-resistant storage in** this rough-textured shower room. **The interior walls are constructed from a grey, non-sanded grout that is applied like plaster – a waterproof material more commonly used as a robust lining for swimming pools. By contrast, the floor of the shower is made of smooth slate.**

Right **A large stone- or slate-clad wet room needs heating to ensure that it is an inviting place to walk into. However, electricity and water are a potentially deadly combination, so any heating or lighting should be installed by a registered professional.**
Far right, top **This simple disc-backed knob can be easily turned to vary the temperature of the water.**
Far right, bottom **An efficient central drain and cover are essential in a wet room. The cover should have closely set ridges so that small items such as bottle tops and caps are not washed away.**

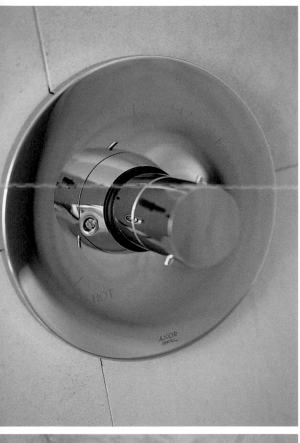

from below the main water tank. In general, the shower head should be installed at a height that suits you, perhaps 15 centimetres above the top of your head. If the shower is for family use, it may be preferable to choose an adjustable head, which can be moved up and down on a pole fixed to the wall to suit the various heights of different members of the family.

Technological advance has made the experience of taking a shower potentially even quicker and more convenient than it used to be. There are now showers available with temperatures and spray patterns that can be pre-selected; there are even timers that can ensure that the shower is ready for use at the right temperature when the alarm clock wakes you up each morning. The Logic Curva enclosure by Vernon Tutbury has a digital display panel on its exterior which gives an exact temperature readout before you venture in. Comfort is also considered to be a crucial part of the showering ritual. You may shower at speed in the morning, but at night you may, if space allows,

Many people find a shower an ideal way to start the day, a blast of water from head to foot, washing away sleepiness and preparing the mind and body for the day.

prefer to sit and linger in the moist and steamy atmosphere. To meet this need, manufacturers have produced wooden and stainless-steel shelf-style benches, seats in perforated plastic and steel bucket shapes, and a ceramic ledge that can be tiled onto a sturdy exterior wall.

Although acrylic, fibreglass and resin mixes are increasingly used in pre-formed units, glass is still popular for the majority of panels and doors. The type used should be British Safety Kitemark, or equivalent, safety glass; for doors and panels this is usually 6 to 8 millimetres thick. The glass is offered in plain or opaque panels and sometimes with decorative motifs or patterns in opaque on a clear background or visa versa. You can also buy opaque glass-effect sticky-back plastic, which can be used to create a design that can then be stuck onto the glass. The plastic should be stuck on the dry, outer side of the glass rather than the moist, inner surface so that the adhesive properties will not be affected. Developments in the production and toughening of glass mean that rounded and frameless walls are now possible without being prohibitively expensive. Among other recent innovations is the glass surface that has been treated so that water rolls off in beads, taking limescale and dirt with it.

Wet rooms

A wet room is simply a shower in a room that has been totally waterproofed. Well established on the Continent, the wet room usually consists of a totally tiled enclosed space with a sloping floor and a central drain. It does away with the problems of damp clingy curtains and the restrictions and confines of a cabinet and allows more than one person to shower at a time.

Wet rooms should be installed under professional supervision because it may be necessary to tank the walls, ceiling and floor with a polythene membrane to prevent leakage. A waste outlet must be sunk into the floor, which needs to slope slightly so that the water is channelled into the outlet.

The shower head can be plumbed in through the wall with a simple dial or taps beneath so that there is minimal gadgetry on show. There will also be plenty of space for a small wooden seat or bench and a sauna bucket filled with back brushes and loofahs on hand for a good all-over scrub.

Right and below **Slate has become an increasingly popular finish for the walls and floors of wet rooms and shower rooms. It can be cut in large squares to reduce the number of joins. Slate also has an interesting surface, with grain and texture. Dry slate is a soft shade of grey but when wet it takes on a deeper charcoal colour. The dark grey contrasts well with greenish glass, silver accessories and pristine white towels.**

Opposite page **Two hinged panels of opaque glass mark the boundaries between the different areas of this bathroom. Separated from the rest of the room by a small door, the lavatory has its own niche, while a larger glass door swings open to give access to the shower. A horizontal surface of poured concrete provides a useful resting place for towels and other accessories while you are having a shower.**

Although the wet room is traditionally an open space, you could build in low walls or benches as part of the floor plan. For example, it is possible to incorporate a low ridge around the back of the showering area so that a small pool of water builds up and you can stand in it up to ankle height. An alternative is a bench-height raised platform, which could be used either to sit on or as a place to put bath products and sponges.

If the wet room is small, it may be sensible to keep towel rails and towels on the wall outside or in a passageway, as stray spray and the build-up of steam may cause the towels to become damp. If the room is large and the ventilation effective, the moisture should disperse without causing problems.

In a wet room where there are a lot of cold tiled surfaces, underfloor or behind-tile wall heating may help take the initial chill off the room. The installation of this type of heating should be done only by a professional electrician in collaboration with a plumber so that they can guarantee that the room is watertight. This is essential for safety and to avoid damage to other parts of the building.

The grout between the tiles in a wet room may become stained if ventilation is inadequate or if your water contains certain salts or chemicals, so try to find a grout that is mould-retardant as well as recommended for holding its original colour. The surface of tiles may also become dull from constant wetting and drying, and deposits may build up, so they will need regular washing and rinsing. Villeroy & Boch have developed the Ceramic Plus surface, which is so smooth that water, dirt and calcium deposits run straight off, leaving it clean and shining.

3
equipment

lighting

fixtures

appliances

furniture

accessories

WHEN YOU KNOW WHAT KIND OF BATHROOM YOU WANT AND HAVE SETTLED ON

THE LIKELY LAYOUT OF THE ROOM, YOU CAN START TO MAKE DECISIONS ABOUT

LIGHTING, FIXTURES, APPLIANCES, FURNITURE AND ACCESSORIES. ALTHOUGH

YOUR CHOICES WILL BE RESTRICTED BY THE SPACE AND MONEY AVAILABLE, THIS

IS WHERE COLOUR, STYLE AND MORE FANCIFUL ELEMENTS CAN COME INTO PLAY –

BUT THEY SHOULD NOT BE AT ODDS WITH THE OVERALL AIM OF MAKING THE

BATHROOM A SAFE, EFFICIENT AND COMFORTABLE PLACE.

There is a bewildering assortment of equipment to choose from, ranging from taps and shower heads to tiles and bathmats. If possible, inspect the item or finish before buying it, or obtain a sample. Objects that look glamorous in a brochure, professionally lit and expertly styled, can lose some of their shine in the cold, hard light of a showroom or newly arrived in your freshly plastered bathroom.

The easiest place to start is with the fixtures because these are the biggest items and usually come in suites, so that the bath, lavatory, handbasin and bidet are in the same or similar shape and with a matching finish. If you have settled on a definite decorative theme, this will influence your choice of shape and colour. For example, an Art Deco scheme might lead you to choose square, angular designs, whereas a contemporary plan could direct you to a freestanding glass basin.

Once the suite has been selected, and checked to ensure that the size and configuration suit your needs, you can chose the ancillary pieces such as the taps or faucets. Walk around a showroom or plumber's merchant and try the various handles until you find one that is comfortable to use and appropriate for your setting. Plumbing requirements might be dictated by the openings drilled into the rim of the bath. For instance, some baths have a single hole for a monobloc fitting, which has a single

spout with the integral taps or levers on both sides. There are other baths that have no tap openings at all because the taps and spout are intended to be wall-mounted – or there may be three separate openings, one for each tap and a third to accommodate a pop-up waste.

Lighting should be carefully planned so that it is functional as well as attractive, and versatile enough to create a variety of moods and settings. Safety considerations must be very carefully adhered to when installing lighting in a bathroom because it is a place where people are often vulnerable and unprotected.

There is not usually much furniture in a bathroom, but a stool can be useful for sitting on to do a pedicure or manicure. An armchair is a restful spot in which to enjoy the warm, relaxed feeling that most people experience after a bath or shower. A linen basket is a practical item that can also be used as a stool, and a linen press or an armoire would be a bonus if you have space for it.

Other accessories will no doubt be influenced by your choice of taps and appliances. For example, if you select a chrome or silvery-coloured finish, then the toothbrush holder, mirror surround and possibly the heated towel rails and other metal-trimmed objects should be of the same finish to give uniformity; this is particularly important in a small room.

Few safety warnings can be more basic but vital in a bathroom: water and electricity are a dangerous, potentially fatal combination. Any electrical work carried out in the bathroom should be done by a professional. The bathroom is also a place where you are often vulnerable, without clothing or shoes that might earth or insulate you from a shock, and your naked skin can be scorched and easily damaged. So, for your own well-being, heed all safety warnings relating to electrical fittings and bathroom lights.

lighting

Any lamps or fittings for use in the bathroom must be specially made for wet places and enclosed in sealed covers or shades to protect them from the effects of steam and condensation. High-voltage lights should be operated only by pull cords, or from outside the bathroom, so that there is no direct contact between wet hands and a switch. You should never use track lighting in a bathroom because of the danger that moisture may come into contact with exposed wiring.

Low-voltage lighting can generally be used safely as long as the bulbs are in enclosed fittings and any sockets are double-insulated. Once the safety factors have been fully comprehended, you can give attention to the creative business of arranging the lighting.

Daylight is the best and cheapest source of illumination. To make the best use of it, you may want to place the handbasin or basins near the window. Natural light also gives a much more realistic idea of skin tone and colour, but no matter how good the natural light in your bathroom you will need to enhance it for shaving or other tasks that involve close scrutiny, as well as at darker times of the day or year.

Different types of artificial lighting

A bathroom needs two main types of artificial lighting: the bright and stimulating kind that gives a good clear vision of what you are doing, and a low relaxing illumination that is soft and subtle. To achieve the right balance between these two requires good planning. You may also find it

Above **The opaque window glass allows daylight to penetrate the room but obscures the view from outside.**
Far right **The long narrow panels diffuse the light from outside as it enters the dark shower enclosure.**

Small picture top **A small window sill can be tiled and used as a shelf.**
Small picture below **Placing a basin beside a window will provide the best access to daylight to assist shaving or the application of make-up.**

useful to have two electrical circuits that can be operated from a panel outside the bathroom and fitted with dimmer switches. Some of these panels can be pre-programmed so that all you have to do is touch the right number for lighting that is bright, mid-level or specifically targeted. In addition to general and targeted lighting, mid-level wall lights can be used to soften and even out shadows cast by overhead lights.

To begin with, you should designate a central ceiling area for a functional or ambient light – an all-purpose illumination that you turn on when you enter the room. It can take the form of a central ceiling light or

integral shaving sockets. For a mirror above the basin, or for a separate dressing or make-up table, there is another way to generate regular, well-balanced illumination – by making an arch or surround of unshaded pearlized light-bulbs in a style associated with the dressing rooms of Hollywood movie stars. The bare bulbs that form part of such an arrangement may seem basic and unfinished, however, and should be installed only in specially designed safety fittings.

Target lighting may also be useful where a lavatory or shower is in a separate cabinet or recessed behind a wall in an area that has insufficient ambient or natural light. The shower enclosure and lavatory can be specifically targeted with downlighters or spotlights.

Other interesting combinations of lighting with an integral secondary feature include a light/ventilator, which is ideal for a small cloakroom or bathroom because the fan or ventilator is activated as soon as the light switch is turned on. Another variation is the light/heater, which can be very useful in small rooms where one wall is an outside wall and a small radiator is either impractical (due to lack of wall space) or inadequate. A light/heater is mounted on a wall above head height and operated by means of a pull cord.

Identifying the right fittings

Even though the selection is limited by safety considerations, there are plenty of bathroom light fittings to choose from. These range from period-inspired lights with opal glass and chrome finishes to central ceiling lights made up of several adjustable arms which can be arranged to make an interesting shape as well as to give a wide pool of light. Wall lights can be round, oblong, diamond-shaped or square, and you may find that an opaque finish gives a softer more diffuse light than clear glass.

A flat disc that screws into a metal plate is not the only type of enclosed shade. There are glass orbs or globes that stand proud of the wall on backplates or adjustable brackets. Angular shades that complement the angular lines of Art Deco fixtures can also be found, as can a flame-like glass shade with a fitting that resembles a torch. Bulkhead fittings, modelled on those used in ships, are both watertight and have nautical overtones that can enhance the utilitarian mood of an industrially inspired chrome bathroom. Although clear or plain glass shades give the most effective light for close scrutiny,

Above **A light shining up through a glass shelf illuminates the bottles and vase above, creating a focal point. Some light will also reflect into the small mirror.**
Right **Recessed ceiling lights are ideal for a bathroom, where all lights should be enclosed. The light from above has been directed to focus on specific areas such as the wall above the mirror and handbasin.**

a central row of recessed downlighters. Recessed down-lighters are a good idea in a bathroom with a low ceiling because, unlike a ceiling light, they won't intrude upon valuable head room. As well as functional lighting you will need task lighting to facilitate shaving, make-up application, flossing of teeth and general maintenance. This should be targeted on the mirror over the hand-basin, where most such activities involving close scrutiny take place.

Task lighting should offer a clean, even, shadow-free illumination. This is best provided by a strip light with a tungsten or fluorescent tube or by two well-placed and well-balanced side lights. Some mirrors have their own built-in lights, and some fluorescent-strip fittings have

Right **Some cabinets and mirrors specifically designed for bathrooms have rows of small lights on either side that cast an even light over the reflection. A combination of lights is used in this bathroom. There are overhead lights recessed into the ceiling, an under-mirror light which illuminates the handbasin and contents of the shelf, and side lights at the edge of the mirror.**

Right, clockwise from top left
Pale shiny walls reflect light, reducing the need for artificial illumination. This magnifying mirror with integral light is ideal for close facial scrutiny. Wall-mounted lights flush to the wall are both useful and decorative – their rounded form complements the shapes of the mirrors and basins. These conical opaque shades let light shine through them as well as below.

coloured shades and tinted bulbs can add a decorative or light-hearted element to the bathroom. Lights with coloured shades or pale-coloured bulbs can be wired on a separate circuit, so that the main circuit operates practical lighting while the secondary one operates the mood lighting, which can be used at bathtime or to enhance a relaxing evening shower.

Creating special effects

After an energetic stint in the bathroom with all the lights blazing, you may want to transform the room into a tranquil haven. This can be done by turning off the central light or central section of downlighters and dimming the outer, perimeter lights. Experiment with different combinations until you find the perfect setting for you, the one that makes you feel most relaxed. For example, you could turn out all the lights except for a spotlight trained on the bath, or leave the bath in darkness and keep on low lights around the perimeter of the room.

A level of illumination that is restful but not too dramatic can be created by using wall lights controlled by a dimmer switch. Some spa and whirlpool baths have lights fitted below the water level so that, when they are lit, the inside of the bath and the swirling water become the focal point in a room where the ambient light has been dimmed. Lights that can be recessed into the floor have thick, ribbed-glass, domed lids that

screw into a metal casing. Such recessed lights can be used to create pools of light up walls, in corners or beside steps leading up to a raised dais area or sunken bath, but they are not advisable in the area of the bathroom used as a main thoroughfare.

Spotlights – ceiling-mounted or secreted behind a shelf or in an appropriate corner – can be used to highlight particular features. The level of light directed at the feature should be at a more intense level than the ambient light in the rest of the room so that the feature stands out.

Candles, especially the scented varieties, have also become a popular source of low-level illumination in the bathroom, but they should be carefully placed so that they are not likely to cause a fire. The effect of the soft yellow flames of candles can be enhanced by placing them in front of a mirror or reflective surface. Although candles are romantic when lit, the after-effect of their flickering flames can be less appealing. In the damp atmosphere of the bathroom the soot emitted from the burning wick can stick to the walls and surfaces, causing a build-up of fine dark powder. This is easy enough to wipe off tiles or similar shiny surfaces but can smear and be difficult to remove effectively from rough plaster and some matt-finish paints. If candles appeal to you, buy a smokeless variety.

A chandelier brings a touch of decadence to an indulgent bathroom. The play of soft muted light on the glass pendants can create rainbows

and star-like bursts. In a room where the ambient light is low and a pin-hole spotlight is directed onto the chandelier, the effect can be luxurious and romantic, even in an otherwise stark setting. Before installing this kind of fitting, check with the supplier that it is suitable for bathroom use.

Safety precautions

If you need to change a lightbulb, ensure that the area around the light fitting is dry. If you are using a step ladder, check that the floor, especially if it is tiled, is dry and not slippery – you should also have someone else with you to hold the ladder steady. The light should be turned off before the bulb is changed – but, if you have a pull switch, it can be hard to be sure about this because there is rarely a visible indication of whether the light was on or off when the bulb failed. In such a case it is sensible to turn off the main electrical circuit until the bulb has been changed.

Some light shades, such as bulkheads and flush ceiling fittings, may require a screwdriver to remove the shade. This can be tricky, and you may need a second pair of hands to help you to complete the operation safely: standing on a ladder, using the screwdriver, catching the screws and holding the shade can be a lot to expect one person to cope with.

If the seal of the shade is effective, the inside should be clean and dust-free. However, if the shade is dirty, take the opportunity to give it a thorough wipe. When replacing the shade, ensure that any seal is neatly replaced and that the whole fixture is screwed or clipped tightly shut. Beware of screwing the glass over tightly or it may crack or break.

Above **A sealed, damp-proof casing is a vital safety feature in a light fixture.** Right **Recessed floor lighting and glass panels create an interesting combination. When the other lights in the room are dimmed, the effect on the glass is even more striking.**

Top right and far right **Uplighters cast dramatic fanlike shafts of light up an old brick wall. Surrounded by smooth pebbles, which echo their rounded shape, the lights are set beside a floor of wooden decking that reflects the linear arrangement of the bricks.**

fixtures

Solid pieces of equipment that are plumbed into a permanent position, fixtures include the bath, handbasin, lavatory and bidet – they come in an ever increasing choice of shapes, finishes and colours. Most sinks, lavatories and bidets are made in glazed ceramic whose smooth, glass-like finish can withstand high temperatures and strong disinfectant cleaners.

In ancient times baths were made from many different materials, including stone and wood. The Victorians favoured heavy cast iron with a glazed enamelled finish on the inside of the tub. The acrylic bath – a discovery of the 1970s – gave rise to a whole range of new designs because it could be easily moulded and coloured. It was also lightweight, easy to move and simple to plumb.

Early acrylic baths were easily scratched and had a tendency to creak and feel unstable because they were relatively flexible; this type of bath is now a much more solid and sturdy part of the bathroom set.

The rise of acrylic-based materials has had a lasting effect on the bathroom. For example, Corian R, made by DuPont – a combination of acrylic resin and natural minerals – is used to form shower trays and integral basins and surfaces. The material is completely solid, non-porous and will not crack, rot or warp. It can be cut, carved, routed, sandblasted, inlaid and thermoformed into a multitude of shapes. Any stains that appear on the surface can be scoured away and accidental cuts and scratches smoothed with fine sandpaper. The material can also be coloured and veined to appear like marble, or incorporated with flecks and fine particles to imitate other stones. It is currently available in around 70 plain colours from the pale to the dark end of the spectrum.

Since the 1990s other mixes of synthetic and natural materials have been developed, creating hybrid surfaces that are warm and light but strong and durable. Quaryl by Ucosan is made from a fusion of acrylic and quartz stone. The product is fully recyclable, has inbuilt noise reduction properties and is resistant to knocks and scratches. Like Corian, Quaryl can be cut and moulded into numerous shapes and forms. Another composite is Ficore by Design & Form, which is claimed to keep water warm six times longer than standard acrylic.

Traditional and modern baths

Some people love the weight and solidness of a classic cast-iron bath, no matter whether it is an original or a reproduction. Genuine old baths may need some work to restore them to their former glory. The cheapest option is to do it yourself with an enamelling kit; this is suitable for covering over a small chip or crack but will be inadequate for correcting

Below **This indulgent bath with its panelled surround has been put in the centre of the room in front of the window so that the bather can admire the view. The tub has double rounded ends and central taps and shower mixer, meaning that the bather can sit in comfort at either end. The wide rim serves as a shelf, allowing bath accessories to be kept close at hand.**

Right and far right **The rolltop bath looks as effective in a modern scheme as in a traditional one. Old cast-iron baths can still be bought through salvage companies but may need re-enamelling. Reproductions are widely available, as are rolltops in lightweight acrylics and synthetic materials.**

Bottom right **If you are fitting an old bath, check that the weight of the bath when full of water will not overburden the floor joists beneath.**

a larger problem. If your bath needs a full-scale respray, there are firms who can send workers to your home to do the job; some will even reposition tap holes to suit modern plumbing requirements – but these companies usually guarantee the new finish for only two years.

For a more permanent and professional finish, the bath can be reconditioned at a workshop or factory. The less expensive option is the infra-red lamp system, which reconditions the bath surface. Alternatively, the bath can be re-enamelled. This long and involved process starts with the removal of the old enamel by sand blasting, followed by respraying and fixing the new enamel in a furnace. The spraying and firing is done about six times so that the finish is immaculate and permanent.

The traditional styles, such as the rolltop, can also be made from pressed steel, which is cheaper and much lighter than cast iron and has a more even surface, so the enamelling results in a better finish. The process for manufacturing pressed steel is more environmentally sound, and after use the bath fabric can be recycled.

Many modern-style baths come in other materials, some returning to the inspiration of the ancient Romans and the Japanese, with tubs in stone or wood. Stainless steel and reinforced glass are also fashionable. Wooden tubs are often made from cypress or teak because those woods have a natural oil which protects the surfaces from the water. Few wooden baths are entirely watertight, so

This sculptural steel bath was custom-made with an undulating base – which allows bathers to sit at the shallow end, to wash their feet, or at the deep end, where they can rest with their legs in a raised position. The design also makes it impossible for the bather to slip down the bath. Baths fashioned from thin sheet metal could cause the water to cool quickly, but most have a double skin that traps air between the two layers, creating a form of insulation and keeping the water warmer for longer.

Above **This standing spout arches gracefully over the side of the bath rather than interrupting its clean, uncluttered lines.**
Above right and far right **Water therapies and spa**

baths are popular, but the plumbing for these machines should be installed to ensure that they are fully drained after each use – otherwise water may rest in the bends and become stagnant.

Below **A towel rail runs all around the outer edge of this bath. It is not only a practical piece of equipment but also a decorative feature that breaks up the bath's plain white sides.**

they should ideally be positioned on a tiled floor with built-in drainage. Many also have to be kept filled with water to prevent the wood from drying out and splitting.

The traditional rolltop was a freestanding bath with claw feet; its side was left black or painted to match the colour of the room. Twenty-first-century versions can be set into a raised plinth to appear sunken, or placed against a wall and enclosed with panels. There are also single- and double-ended options in which both ends are rounded or one is rounded and the other left square.

Modern manufacturers have emulated the rolltop but given their baths a more contemporary styling. Philippe Starck's design is a freestanding oval bath with a thick flat rim and an optional towel rail running just underneath the rim. There are also designs that come with enamelled finishes both inside and out and are raised on an external frame of chrome legs and bars.

Another old-fashioned classic bath that can be found in reproduction is the Slipper bath, which has a high raised end, like a hip bath, and a lower rounded end.

Standard baths are generally single- or double-ended and come with an optional apron or side panel used to conceal the pipes and plumbing. Alternatively, you can have your own panel constructed from tongue and groove, wood or whatever suits your scheme. Usually cheaper than cast iron, acrylic baths have insides that come in a number of different styles: some are plain, while others are slightly sculpted with shaped sides and a slope going down to the base; there are even baths shaped in a figure of eight that narrows in the centre and opens out at each end.

Baths designed to cope with over-bath showers have a wider end to allow more room for movement and a shower curtain or glass panel. Short and small baths with tapered sides have been specifically designed for small spaces, and there are also extra-large and extra-deep baths available. A bigger bath will be heavier and take more water than a smaller one – so, if you are tempted, check that your joists and floorboards are up to supporting the total weight.

Handbasins

Handbasins come in various sizes and shapes and can be wall-hung, placed on a pedestal or set into a vanity unit. When deciding on the size and shape of your

handbasin, consider how often you use it and what for. If the basin is in a cloakroom and used only for washing your hands, it does not have to be particularly big. Deep basins are necessary only if you need a substantial volume of water.

Many basins come with a pedestal. This not only provides a place for the bowl to rest but can also be used to disguise the pipework, which can be run down behind the recess in the back. The disadvantage of a pedestal is that it gives you little choice about the height at which the basin is installed.

Wall-mounted basins can be plumbed in at a height to suit you, but the piping will need to be led out behind the basin in a special covering. Corner basins do not often come with pedestals because they are usually set on brackets that are fixed to the two

Opposite page, far left **The antique basin in a metal column base with a fold-over lid is more for show than regular use. It would be an attractive and unusual talking point in any bathroom.**

Opposite page, left **This sleek streamlined trough basin is inspired by the sort of sink that doctors and nurses used to scrub up in, and the lever taps can be turned on and off with the forearm rather than the hands, but it is ideal in a bathroom where a basin is required only for hand and teeth washing.**

Left **Cast-concrete basins such as this one can be constructed to size so that they will fit into narrow or difficult spaces.**

Above **The classic white ceramic sink is still universally popular and works well in most decorative schemes.**

long sides of the basin structure and secured to the walls on both sides. Some basins are semi-inset into a surround with the back part slotted into a shelf or cupboard and the front section standing proud. The space around the basin is used for a soap dish or bathroom products.

An alternative is the fully inset sink, in which the bowl is set wholly into a surface, often of marble or glass. Some inset sinks are edged with a lip or rim that sits on top of the surface. Others have an unglazed rim that sits directly under the opening; the unglazed rim creates a flat, neat seam with the upper surface so that there is no gap for water to run through.

A fashionable option for a basin is the bowl and wash-table effect – apparently a freestanding separate bowl resting on a table or glass shelf. This clean and simple look is reminiscent of the traditional bowl and jug used in homes before modern plumbing was invented. The modern bowl has a central waste outlet and the tap – because it is usually a single sculptural monobloc and lever – is plumbed to one side, with the spout over the edge of the bowl.

Another modern development is the freestanding basin built into a tall-legged frame that incorporates towel rails, soap and toothbrush holders, a shelf and mirror. This also has a faintly period look that can be traced back to the Victorian washstand combined with a gentleman's valet stand. Another modern design is the Washington basin, which consists of two

Below **Metal basins need to be carefully maintained. The surface should be finished with a lacquer or varnish to prevent tarnish and rust.**

Above far left **This stone sink has a smooth rounded front and two small earlike platforms on which to put soap. In contrast with the old and rustic style of the sink, the taps are modern levers with a single spout.**
Below far left **A glass sink in a steel ring support is ideal for a streamlined or smaller bathroom; its delicate appearance means that it will not seem bulky in a small space. The wall-mounted taps and spout are positioned at a good height above the bowl so that they do not get in the way while you are washing.**
Left **The ceramic bowl on a shelf support is reminiscent of the times before bathrooms were plumbed in, when freestanding bowls were filled with water from a jug.**
Right **Square or oblong sinks are well suited to a bathroom with an angular or geometric scheme.**

concentric stainless-steel spheres. The outer bowl with the waste outlet is fixed, but the inner bowl, which pivots, holds the water while it is being used. When washing is completed the inner bowl is tipped so that the water can run out through the waste outlet in the fixed underbowl.

Glass basins are another fashionable feature most often seen in architect-designed homes. These basins look spectacular but they are expensive and some have to be individually made. Also, being a fashionable concept, they may date quickly.

Lavatories

The old-fashioned style of lavatory has a raised cistern with a pan at the end of the metal flush pipe. The overhead cistern is flushed by means of a chain and handle. These lavatories look appropriate as part of a traditional themed bathroom but take up wall space and are difficult to clean thoroughly because there are so many parts.

The close-coupled lavatory is probably the most common style, with the cistern attached to the pan by a wide trunk at the back of the pan. This is a practical, no-nonsense style of lavatory, but it can take a long time to clean because there are three visible parts: the cistern, the join

Top, above and far right **The finishing touches and details should be in keeping with the overall style and colour scheme of the room. For example, these simple understated levers are appropriate partners for unfussy fixtures in a modern streamlined bathroom.**

Right and centre top **A ceramic or wooden hand pull suspended from a chain is needed to maintain the integrity of this old-fashioned high-level flush lavatory.**

and the pan. In the least obtrusive type of lavatory, the pan is attached directly to the wall and the cistern, generally a plastic one, is concealed behind a false wall. The cistern has to be at a minimum of 800 millimetres above the floor to enable a satisfactory flush, and the pan is usually wall-hung, but there are some designs that come with a foot or pedestal.

There are also two options when it comes to flushing the lavatory. One is the basic open-rim method, when water is propelled by the strength of the flush along the upside-down, U-shaped rim at the edge of the bowl. The other method is the box rim, where the water is carried in a tube with punched holes in the underside so that the water is evenly and thoroughly distributed. The box rim offers the more thorough cleaning system, and is usually quieter.

If you have a small bathroom where a macerator lavatory seems to be the most appropriate choice, remember to be careful what you throw down it. The macerator is not designed to cope with wads of cotton wool after you have removed your make-up; these should be put in a wastepaper basket and thrown out with the general rubbish. The other thing about a lavatory in a small space is that the ventilation must be efficient enough to ensure that odours do not linger.

Manufacturers are increasingly conscious of the need to keep water and energy consumption to a minimum. The flush facility on a lavatory used to be a standard 7.5 litres, but developments in water-saving technology mean that the volume has now been reduced to 6 litres, which will soon be the new statutory limit in the UK.

Bidets

A much underrated piece of bathroom equipment, the bidet has long been part of the standard bathroom in continental Europe but has been slower to become established in the UK. The bidet is a boon to personal hygiene and comfort, and can be particularly useful if you have young children, who may need to be washed regularly when in the early stages of toilet training.

Bidets also provide relief for people who suffer from medical complaints such as haemorrhoids and for elderly people who find a full bath or shower too difficult as a daily activity. Bidets are either floor-standing or wall-hung; if they are wall-hung, the weight should be supported by a concealed pair of strong aluminium brackets.

Top **A Philippe Starck tap gives the finishing touch to this pair of fixtures – an ultra-modern, wall-hung bidet and lavatory. Bidets are available in a wide range of styles made to match the lavatory and the other items in the suite. There is also a variety of taps and spouts to choose from. Some people would never be without a bidet, but others cannot see the point of them.**

Left **The classical style of bidet provides an attractive and practical addition to a wide range of white suites.** Above **The old-fashioned slipper design has retained its popularity.**

appliances

Modern appliances are manufactured not only to be attractive and functional but also to take account of the need to save energy and water. However, safety remains the most important feature of any appliance in a bathroom.

Environmental considerations have led manufacturers to develop taps that help to conserve water by mixing it with air. The process – described as aerating – reduces the amount of water used without decreasing the power of the water flow.

Sensor technology also helps to save water. Instead of taps that you turn on manually and may leave running, or taps that you do not turn off properly, with the result that they drip, the device turns on the water only if it is activated by the movement of a hand under the sensor. Lavatories are also being adapted to operate with a smaller volume of water.

At the moment sensor technology is found most commonly in airport washrooms and hotels, but it will soon be more widespread in domestic bathrooms. Until that time manually operated taps remain the principal way of getting access to water.

Taps

The most traditional sort of tap is the pillar tap, usually found in pairs – one for hot water and the other for cold. In the classic arrangement each tap has a knob on top for turning the water on and off and individual spouts for the water to flow through.

The pillar tap can also be used in a three-hole basin mixer, in which there are separate hot and cold turning functions but no individual spouts; the water is channelled instead through a central spout.

An alternative to this arrangement is the monobloc mixer, which consists of a central spout with integral hot and cold taps attached on either side and a lever at the back of the spout that can be raised or lowered to operate the waste disposal outlet.

Bath taps are available in similar styles to basin taps but tend to be bigger. Bidet taps are usually of

Top, far left **Fashioned out of utilitarian copper piping, this tap was made to accompany a square ceramic basin salvaged from a laboratory.**
Top, centre **This long-spout lever tap with a ceramic cap on the handle would suit a white ceramic basin or rolltop bath.**
Above **Pillar taps are usually brass but reproductions may also be found in chrome or nickel. Modern brass taps are usually finished with a varnish or lacquer which prevents them from staining and retains the glossy finish.**

Combining old-fashioned styles with modern technology, taps and spouts can be made to resemble those used in Victorian or Edwardian times but without the problems of leaking washers. Typical of this design is the domed ceramic cap, which often gives the manufacturer's name as well as indicators for hot and cold. The style and size of this arrangement suits the deep white ceramic basin with scalloped back.

the monobloc variety with a pop-up waste, and the spout is often shorter than those found in a handbasin; sometimes it includes a directional spray nozzle.

The knob or handle part of the tap comes in many forms. Choose a shape that feels comfortable in your hand and a colour that complements the rest of the metalwork in your bathroom.

There are no rules about pairing traditional taps with a classic bath or modern taps with a modern bath, but in general the simpler the combination of styles the better. Traditional designs include crossbar taps, usually available in chrome or brass, and often including ceramic discs

nickel. This has a softer look than more conventional designs and gives the impression that the taps are icy cold with condensation. Standard appliances such as a pillar tap with a solid knob that is wider at the top and tapers down to the tap combines elements of classic and modern styles. The knob has indented curves in four sections so that it is easier to grip and turn than a tap with a totally smooth shape. This knob is also available in ceramic finishes that are tinted to co-ordinate with bath and basin colours.

Philippe Starck has designed some curved lever taps that taper slightly at the top and bottom, which gives them an almost feather-like appearance. In his Starck range the design is further simplified so that a single lever tap and a mono mixer spout with lever-operated waste outlet form a single sculptural pillar.

The shape of modern spouts has become smoother and more rounded so that they arc over the basin. Some of the levers that operate both the water flow and waste outlet are

printed with the words 'hot' and 'cold'. Victorian crossbar taps tarnish without regular polishing; the modern brass finishes are often sealed to prevent this. Although modern copies of traditional taps may look old-fashioned, they incorporate the latest technology, such as a quarter-turn facility that makes the tap more responsive to your touch.

In addition to the crossbar taps there are ceramic-covered lever taps that have a similarly old-fashioned appeal. The operating mechanism is opened by pushing the lever from one side to the other. A disadvantage with lever taps is that it is harder than with normal taps to ensure that you have turned them off properly.

As an alternative to the traditional chrome and brass finishes, you can give a classic tap such as the crossbar a more contemporary look with a matt finish such as satin

sleekly slimline, resembling a fine metal rod with small, rounded, button-like ends for easier grip. The two most common options for waste cover are the pop-up and the plug and chain. There is also an overflow outlet in case the bath is mistakenly left running – if this happens, the water that reaches near the top is siphoned off to prevent overflowing. The overflow is generally a disc with six round holes to which a plug and chain may be attached. The other choice is a smooth round disc with a concealed semicircular opening at the base; this is usually found in conjunction with a pop-up waste outlet.

Shower controls and heads

Single thermostatic control valves for showers can be operated with either a disc or handle that can be turned from the cold to the hot side of the dial until you find the right temperature. Dual-control thermostatic valves have two functions: one regulates the heat; the other the flow of water. Most of these controls allow you to pre-set the temperature so that you can simply walk into the shower and turn it on – there is no guessing and manipulating until you get it right. The dual-control panel is similar to the single one but

Opposite page, far left **The industrial-style, wall-mounted, triangular-headed taps with S-shaped spouts were chosen to harmonize with the narrow, trough-like basin.**

Opposite page, left **A simple lever-action basin mixer supplies mixed hot and cold water through the spout; the lever also regulates the rate of flow.**

Above left **The distinctive Starck three-piece basin mixer with the smooth and sculptural lever taps has been plumbed in through the basin surround.**

Above **An arc spout rears up in front of the plunge-operated waste outlet. The plunge is depressed to lift the cover to the waste outlet and raised to close it. The cap of the waste outlet is usually a smooth dome which fits neatly into the base of the basin or bath.**

shower, so the water will reach you no matter what height you are. Shower heads are also available in a variety of sizes and shapes. The disc diameters of the traditional shower rose range from 12 to 30 centimetres, but check with your plumber that your water pressure is strong enough to supply a large rose with a steady supply of water – otherwise you may as well settle for a rose that is small but efficient.

There are many adjustable shower heads on the market that offer a choice of sprays. The water in this type of head is often aerated, which gives it a bubblier quality – although such a system reduces the amount of water required, it does not compromise water pressure. You can gently manipulate the head of a variable shower until it reaches the desired type of spray; the range includes full-force spray, intermediate and concentrated needle spray. One final option is the traditional-style flexible hose and shower head attached to the taps which can be

Left The upper, fixed shower head supplies a broad spray of water at a constant level, while the lower one can be adjusted so that the flow of water varies from heavy massage strength to a light sprinkle. In some cases it may be necessary to install a pump to create enough pressure for a good flow of water.

Opposite page, clockwise from top centre
A modern flexible shower head with fine spray.
A traditional-style concealed shower control.
A thermostatic temperature control – the hot and cold water are supplied from separate inlets but exit through one outlet; the smaller knob is the

open-and-close device used to operate the waste outlet.
A traditional rigid shower rose.
Detail of a shower head on a flexible hose.
A traditional crosshead tap.
This classic bath/shower mixer with lever is sometimes called a telephone fitting because of its resemblence to an old-fashioned Bakelite telephone.
A four-tap bath/shower mixer with a single metal spout – two of the taps supply water for the bath; the other two supply the shower head above.
Centre **A modern dual-control thermostatic valve – one knob regulates the flow of water, the other the water temperature.**

has two knobs or levers, or sometimes inner and outer discs. Shower heads are either fixed or flexible. A fixed head that comes with its own integral arm can be fitted directly to the wall or attached to a separate shower arm. It can be plumbed in at a height that suits the person who will be using it, and the plumbing and pipes may be concealed in the wall.

A sliding bar is useful for people who like to be able to change the height of the shower head. The bar is a pole attached to the wall – the head and a flexible hose can be moved up and down it and secured at the desired height by a clip or screw.

Another option is the needle-spray shower. This is a wrap-around tubular shower that resembles a garden arbour made from piping. The water comes from above and from all of the five circular pipes in the

plumbed into the side or at end of the bath, or on a single, rigid pipe standing beside the bath. This type of shower is fine for a quick rinse or for washing your hair, but it is not ideal for regular daily showering.

Ventilation

When the business of bathing or showering has been completed, the steam and moisture that has been generated should be expelled as swiftly and efficiently as possible. A build-up of steam and condensation can lead to damp surfaces and the possible growth of mould or fungus. It may also give rise to unpleasant damp smells and cause damage to wooden furniture, panelling and accessories. It is generally not enough simply to open the window. You will have to fit an extractor fan, but how large and

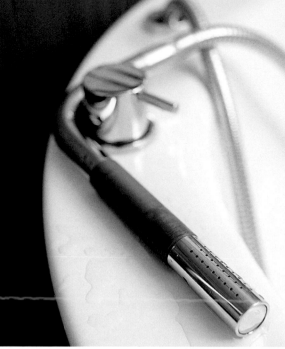

powerful a fan you need depends on the size of your bathroom. The cheapest method of mechanical ventilation is the simple plastic fan fixture that can be set into the top of the bathroom window. This can be activated by pulling an on/off cord.

If you are buying a fan for bathroom use, it is important to choose an extractor rather than a re-circulator. The purpose of the fan is to disperse any moisture and unpleasant smells, not to recycle them around the room.

An extractor system extracts the air – that is, removes it from the room – so you need to provide a route by which replacement fresh air can enter. This can be achieved by installing a grille in the window or by inserting a ventilation brick in an exterior wall, if the bathroom has one.

Before purchasing a fan, establish how much noise it is likely to make. This is particularly important if your bedroom is next door to the bathroom – the whirring of the fan and the motor could keep you awake for half an hour after a night-time visit to the bathroom – so ask for a demonstration of the fan in the showroom.

Electrical appliances

For safety reasons, electrical appliances other than those specifically designed to work in an insulated low-voltage shaver socket, such as certain items that need recharging, should not be brought into the bathroom.

If you enjoy hearing the radio news while you are in the shower, or listening to music while wallowing in the bath, arrange to have loudspeakers wired into the wall or ceiling and an enclosed select panel placed by the doorway. Otherwise you will have to rely on a battery-operated CD or radiocassette player.

Heating

Old-fashioned radiators that bulge out from the wall are almost a thing of the past in the bathroom. They have been replaced by underfloor heating, which provides ambient heat without taking up precious space, used in conjunction with heated towel rails.

As well as the thermostatically controlled heating elements that run under the floor, there are systems such as trench radiators that slot in level with the floor in a band at the wall's edge. There are convection radiators that can be recessed into the floor or wall-mounted and run off the hot-water system, and panel radiators that are thin, plain and unobtrusive and can be recessed into a wall so that the finished effect is that of an architectural panel.

The panel radiator can be adapted for use as a towel rail by clipping rails or pegs over its frame. Buy ones that are specifically designed to work on your radiator; ordinary plastic hooks may melt and adhere to the panel.

Serpentine curved radiators give a sculptural dimension to a bathroom. The Hot Spring radiator, inspired by a book ring-binder, was designed by Paul Priestman and provides a vertical, pillar-like source of heat which is a feature in its own right. Other coiled radiators finish at the top in a ball finial that can be used to hang up a bathrobe.

Wall-mounted horizontal pipes, evenly spaced or staggered in groups of four bars, can add to the visual interest in a bathroom as well as providing an efficient source of heat. Standard copper piping bent into a large double curve can also be an unusual but practical feature on a bathroom wall. Whatever your preferred radiator, ensure that it is in an area where you are unlikely to touch it accidentally with your bare skin.

Above and below **A heated towel rail fixed to the wall is an invaluable bathroom accessory. Towel rails occupy a minimal amount of space and perform a dual function: they provide heating for the room and offer a means of drying damp towels and other items. The rungs of the ladder-style heaters shown here are often spaced in groups to make it more straightforward to hang things up to dry and also to give the heaters a more interesting, attractive appearance. This type of radiator is available in a wide variety of colours, ranging from the traditional silver/chrome to white and black, as well as a rainbow assortment of coloured enamel finishes.**

Opposite page, far left **A plunger waste control has been teamed here with an equally old-fashioned crosshead chrome tap.**
Opposite page, top **Concealed valves are a feature of these wall-mounted lever taps and spout.**

Opposite page, middle **These stylized taps and spout with a retractable, flexible shower are mounted onto the bath surround.**
Opposite page, foot **A wall-mounted bath spout and valves in chrome with rounded tap heads.**

Heated towel rails

Specially designed heated towel rails are not generally powerful enough in themselves to provide adequate heat in a bathroom, but they have the effect of topping up the ambient heat supplied by underfloor heating or a radiator. They are also useful for drying and warming towels and other items.

Most heated towel rails obtain their power from a central-heating or hot-water system, although there are some that can be heated electrically – but these tend to be less efficient.

The most popular type of heated towel rail is the traditional ladder-style rail finished in chrome, nickel or gold effect. The ladder rail is commonly available in the form of a simple freestanding design or as a wall-mounted version.

Another option, based on the ladder style, is a double-sided rail with an arched top and two sides of rails, back and front. The double rail provides more space for spreading out towels and for the air to circulate around them and promote drying. An alternative to the arch top is the square top, which allows the towels to be fanned out over the lower rails. Simple modern heated rails follow the ladder-style design, but whereas the predominant joints are a feature of the old style, the modern version is a smooth, seamless shape. A simple angular S-shaped rail is also available which provides three horizontal bars for towels.

A narrow three-bar vertical heated towel rail can be used in small spaces. This type of fitting is ideal in a gap between the handbasin and lavatory – a space too tight for a conventional horizontal radiator. What this style of heater lacks in width it makes up for in height, and the overall area emitting heat is comparable to that of the horizontal version.

The concept of the designer towel rail has grown out of the development of the radiator. No longer purely functional appliances, towel rails are now designed in a range of interesting shapes, from cross-over X styles to bow-fronted arcs. They are also available in a range of different colours. No longer confined to the space under the window, they can be found standing pillar-like up the full height of a wall or as a brightly coloured panel in an otherwise plainly decorated room.

Far left **This Cobra-therm radiator offers several cross bars on which towels can be hung to dry or air. It is available in a range of sizes.** Above left **A cobra radiator on a swing mount allows the air to circulate around it freely, not only to warm the air in the room but also to encourage the evaporation of moisture from used towels.** Above **A panel radiator has been set into a recess and a towel rail positioned above it so that anything hanging from the rail benefits from the heat. Placing the radiator in the recess reduces the likelihood of its causing burns by coming into contact with bare skin.**

furniture

Styles in bathroom furniture have changed radically from the days of built-in cabinets that mimicked those in the kitchen – where the look had also become very rigid. There is now a strong preference for freestanding simplicity with minimal clutter.

In the 1970s and 1980s the vogue for creating fitted cupboards and units in melamine with countersunk handbasins and for boxing in the sides of the bath gave bathrooms a somewhat monotonous sameness. Materials, including laminates and panelled doors, also came to resemble those used in the kitchen, but lighter, pastel shades were favoured in the bathroom, and faux marble was preferred to simulated pine.

The trend is now towards a more open feel. Of the few items of furniture found in the bathroom, most are made of real wood and marble or composites of acrylic with marble or stone powder. Where before there might have been a wall of cupboards there may now be only one or two; these are often well constructed from a natural material and finished with plain paint or lacquer that almost merges with the wall colour so that they become invisible.

Tall storage cupboards, reaching from the ceiling to the floor, can be disguised behind panels without any obvious opening device. The cupboard door appears to be part of a wall, but you can push it to activate a spring mechanism that opens the door to reveal the shelves or hanging space inside.

The interest in simplicity and minimalism can be seen in the work of a number of designers – for example, the understated square wooden table that supports the Philippe Stark washing bowl, and the fine pillar-like columns found in Dieter Sieger's Bagnella range. The trend is also clear in the rise of the wall-hung basin, bidet and toilet and the decline of the boxy cupboards and traditional pedestal supports that were once the main forms of support for handbasins.

Some modern bathroom fixtures are actually designed to look like pieces of furniture. For example, there is a piece called the Richmond console basin, which has two

Opposite page, top far left **The classic appearance of these wood-panelled cupboards complements the reception-room style of decoration. The black marble surround and splashback, the bust and glass vase, framed paintings and gilt-framed mirror give the room a formal feel.**

Opposite page, top left **Round knobs are preferable to angular ones at lower levels of the bathroom, where you might bump into them and bruise or hurt yourself.**

Opposite page, bottom **These tall panelled doors conceal ample shelf space where linens can be stored, but in a room where steam and moisture are a daily presence there must be good ventilation to prevent the linens themselves from becoming damp.**

Left and below left **Items of furniture in this room – a double-door cupboard and a cabinet in a similar style under the basin – have been painted white, the** same colour as the walls, so that they blend into the background of this small bathroom, rather than assuming a dominant role.

Below **This bathroom cum dressing room incorporates shelves for towels and sheets, and hanging space for clothes, as well as drawers and cupboards under the basin and vanity unit. Dressing is given more prominence than washing in the decor of this compact but well-designed room.**

shapely turned legs like a conventional console table that you might find in a hallway, but the legs of the Richmond are ceramic, as are its top and countersunk basin.

Where fixed or built-in furniture is found in the modern bathroom it tends to be in the classic style, based on Biedermeier or even Mackintosh. It is frequently made from a wood that has either been stained or left natural, but varnished or sealed. The glossy laminates have also been replaced.

Where formerly there might have been a laminated surround to a basin, it is now more common to find that the sink is an integral part of the surround and raised splashback, and that all the elements are made from the same material. This may be steel, perhaps, or one of the resin composites such as Corian R or Quaryl.

The ability to mould these continuous single pieces means that there are no joins, cracks or crevices for water to trickle down, and that the surfaces can be wiped clean much more easily. The silhouette of the furniture that supports this type of basin has, as a result, also become more streamlined.

Another feature of the modern bathroom is incorporated furniture. This differs from the built-in variety in that it is sculpted as an integral part of the wall or setting rather than conceived as a unit built up against the wall.

Incorporated furniture embraces such items as a curved seat built out on a base from the wall and butting up against the side of the shower. It could also include one or two steps set against the wall in a wet room – these may be tiled or covered in plaster with a waterproof

finish that matches the finish of the main wall or floor, but they are seen as part of the structure of the room rather than as a piece of prefabricated furniture.

Old pieces in new settings

There has also been a long-standing tradition of countersinking handbasins into existing pieces of furniture such as a Victorian marble-topped kitchen cupboard or an Edwardian chest of drawers – even architects' plan chests have been used. This type of unit is often used in a bathroom that has an indulgent decorative theme, and if the furniture is in a particularly attractive style or colour of wood it may be echoed in a wooden lavatory seat or a chair.

Glass-fronted chests of drawers once seen in haberdashery stores are among the old pieces of furniture that have found a place in the modern bathroom. The glass panel at the front of the cabinet means that its contents can be clearly seen, and its tall, slender shape is timeless and unobtrusive but offers plenty of storage space. Old armoires are also found, sometimes stripped of paint and left in their natural wood colour, or limed or washed to give them a pale, clean finish.

Many of these classic pieces of furniture appear less chunky and heavy than fitted units because they have legs, which means that you can see underneath them. Built-in units usually have a plinth base to cover their adjustable metal legs. Filling in the gap between the base of the cupboard and the floor gives the piece a more solid and fixed appearance, whereas light passes beneath an old-fashioned cupboard and makes it seem less permanent.

Opposite page **The attractive shape of this conical unit makes it a feature in the overall decorative scheme. The cabinet doors require no knobs or handles because a magnetic spring catch inside each of them can be released by gently pushing on the door itself. Closing a door is equally simple – you simply bring it back into contact with the magnetic catch, which will hold it until it is released again.**

Top right **The plainer and more streamlined the cupboard doors in a bathroom the fewer niches and crannies there are to collect dust.**
Centre right **Convenient D-handles are used to slide open the shelves of this capacious cabinet.**
Bottom right **Storage space in this bathroom consists of a carefully thought-out combination of drawers and open shelves.**

Shaker-style bathrooms are characterized by simple but well-crafted wooden furniture. In this case the style is traditional but the manufacture is modern. Many companies will build Shaker-style units to order so that they can be tailor-made to fit around awkward plumbing or in spaces that cannot accommodate a standard-sized unit.

The simple panelled doors and uncomplicated lines of the Shaker style can help to create the impression of an efficient no-nonsense bathroom, but the mellow colour of the natural wood or a soft wash of traditional Shaker shades of blue or red gives a more indulgent and homely feel than other starker and more streamlined designs.

Cupboards

Storage is especially important in the streamlined or Zen-style bathroom because the minimalist look requires the room to be free of clutter. There are also safety reasons for avoiding clutter in that it reduces the danger of tripping and sliding or slipping on objects left on the floor or at the edge of a surface. Rather than a couple of small cupboards, you may find that

Opposite page, far left
Bathroom cupboards and storage units should ideally have smooth and rounded handles, which are less likely than angular ones to cause bruising if someone bumps against them.
Centre **This dressing table has a wavelike sculptural quality that enhances the comfortable and soothing character of the bathroom.**
Above left **If a bathroom is also used as a dressing or laundry room, clothes and bedlinen may be stored there, but you should make sure that any build-up of steam and condensation can be swiftly and effectively dispersed; if ventilation is poor, the clothes may become damp and mouldy.**
Below left **By subdividing drawers into smaller spaces, you can increase the number of items they hold.**

one large one will do the job and take up less floor space because the storage area is confined to one tall, narrow unit rather than two or more small and wide ones. The most common place to put a cupboard is under the handbasin, but the new styles and designs of basins – which may incorporate column supports and delicate table-like structures – could mean that storage space will have to be found elsewhere.

The storage of medicines should be carefully planned to ensure that they are kept under lock and key and well out of the reach of children. Even a medicine cabinet high up on a wall will not deter a curious child from climbing up onto a stool to have a look inside. Bleach and any other toxic detergents should also be stored in a secure place.

Seats and day beds

If you need to sit down in a bathroom, it is much more comfortable to be able to use a seat rather than trying to balance on the thin hard rim of the bath. The most suitable type of chair or stool depends on the size and style of room. A simple but sturdy stool can also

be helpful for small children to stand on, so that they can wash their hands at an adult-height handbasin, and to allow toddlers to reach the lavatory with ease – but such a stool must be of the sturdy four-legged variety, and it should be used only under adult supervision.

In a wet room, steam room or good-sized shower room a simple slatted wooden stool can be a bonus. In the steam room you can either sit on the stool or, if the room is large enough, lie down and use the stool to raise your foot above shoulder level – which is both relaxing and said to be beneficial to blood circulation. In a shower or wet room the stool can also be used as a table for setting down soap, shampoo or loofah or as somewhere to sit when washing your feet.

In a good-sized bathroom a chair can be used to put clothes or towels on while you are luxuriating in the bath, or to sit on while you are applying nail varnish or carrying out a pedicure. As the chair may be the only freestanding piece of furniture in the room, and therefore a point of interest, it should be attractively designed and well finished as well as in harmony with the rest of the decoration.

If the bathroom is large enough, a day bed or chaise is an indulgent accessory. In a streamlined or minimalist room this type of furniture is acceptable if the structure itself is very simple – perhaps a wooden bench with a futon or thin cushion on top or a stone slab, like a Hamam massage block, with a padded towelling cover. There are also a number of classic design pieces that would be appropriate in a simple uncluttered setting.

Opposite page **Built-in cabinets provide appropriate storage in a small bathroom. Here the mirrored cupboard has been fitted into a recess above the basin with a convenient shelf beneath.** Left **Deep, narrow shelves slotted into in an otherwise wasted space can have all sorts of uses in a bathroom that is also used for dressing.** Right **Some freestanding fixtures, such as this basin, closely resemble traditional pieces of furniture.**

Examples include Jasper Morrison's Three sofa, which has straight ends but the interior curls and undulates, almost like a body shape, to form two seats. The bent laminated wood and webbing of Alvar Aalto's Model 43 would also be suitable in a bathroom setting because the shape is clean and simple, and the webbing structure will dry easily if it becomes damp. Marcel Breuer's aluminium slatted reclining chair No 313 with beech armrests is ideal because it has no fabric or upholstery that is vulnerable to water damage.

A day bed in an indulgent style of bathroom could be a classic Victorian chaise longue, an old dentist's or barber's chair with leather upholstery and chrome fittings or the classic Le Corbusier recliner. However, you need to be cautious about using upholstered furniture in a bathroom because the humidity may affect not only the fabric covering of the chair or bed but also the stuffing or padding in the seat and back. Try to position any upholstered furniture as far away from the bath or shower as possible and make sure that the room is thoroughly ventilated after every use.

Furniture specially designed to withstand damp or wet conditions, such as garden or beach furniture, may be useful in a bathroom. Plastic garden seats and recliners are not usually particularly attractive, and can be very sweaty to sit on, but the classic wood and canvas director's chair is an option – it has the advantage of being lightweight and foldable so that it can be stored out of the way when not needed, and the canvas dries quickly if it becomes damp.

The classic liner chair with footrest made its way to dry land from the ocean-going ships of the 1930s and 1940s. The modern versions are equally stylish and should be made of treated or well-varnished wood that can cope with the temperatures and

Above **A wicker and wood chair with simple arms looks inviting but may need to be draped with a towel before you sit on it – otherwise the pattern from the seat will be impressed on your skin. Freestanding furniture can add to the comfort and relaxation of the bathing and showering ritual.**
Right **Rather than balancing on one foot or perching on the cold narrow rim of a bath, it is easier to perform a pedicure or manicure when sitting in a suitable chair. Doing your hair or applying make-up is also easier and more comfortable when you have the benefit of a dressing table.**

Opposite page, top **In stream-lined bathrooms and shower rooms a simple stool or table tray may suffice. You can put all the lotions, oils, soaps and other accessories you might want on the tray and take it to where it is needed. If you choose a wooden tray, make sure that it has a water-resistant finish so that it will not warp as a result of frequent exposure to water.**
Opposite page, bottom **This simple slat stool can serve as a table as well as being used as a seat in a shower or sauna.**

or cabinet with a mirror for applying make-up or for checking that your tie or collar is straight. Such an item of furniture has the bonus of providing additional storage space, allowing you to put some of the objects that might have rested on the basin surround on the top of the dressing table or in its upper drawers.

This area will also be useful for keeping odd bits of jewellery that can sometimes accumulate around a handbasin. Watches, rings and earrings are common culprits. If the surface of the dressing table is wooden, use glass or ceramic dishes to protect the finish from the damp bases of bottles and the acid effects of perfumes and aftershave lotions.

Trolleys

Trolleys are mobile shelves on wheels. Many of the units illustrated in fashionable magazines and interiors supplements come from medical establishments such as hospitals and dental surgeries. The simple chrome legs, resting on castors or rubber-trimmed wheels, support glass or metal shelves, which are lightweight and easy to wipe clean.

Trolleys make it simple to move shampoos, bath products, towels and sponges from beside the bath to the shower enclosure or the handbasin as and when they are needed. This means that you only have to have one set of bath products rather than three separate sets – one for each area of the room in which you might choose to wash.

conditions of a bathroom. A liner seat is usually made of wood, so you may need to put some padding over the frame to make it more comfortable – a cushion of this sort should be removable so that it can be taken outdoors to air or dry.

Dressing tables

If you have an en suite bathroom or one that doubles as a dressing room, the style of furniture that you choose for the bathroom should be sympathetic in style and finish to that used in the linking or adjacent rooms, to create a feeling of unity and purpose. In a dressing room or an en suite bathroom you may want to have a traditional dressing table

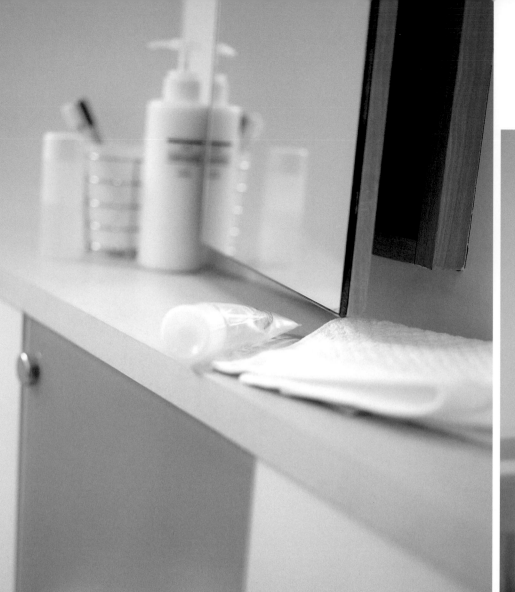

Above and above right **A mirror is an essential piece of bathroom kit. This one has been placed on the front of a recessed cabinet. The mirror appears to have been hung directly onto the wall but it is in fact concealing useful storage space.**

Right **Wherever possible, store cotton wool, tissues and other cosmetic items that are left on show in covers or holders that resemble each other.**

Far right **If you have space, bottles of oil or bath salts can make an attractive display.**

134 Equipment

accessories

In the streamlined bathroom accessories should be kept to a minimum. Only items used on a daily basis should be allowed to stay on open shelves and surfaces. In the indulgent bathroom a few more objects may be put on show, but not so many that the room appears cluttered and untidy. There are some accessories that no bathroom should be without – including a mirror and a lavatory seat.

Oils and other bath preparations may be left on show in the bathroom, but for display it is a good idea to decant them into matching bottles or containers that have a similar appearance. The containers should also co-ordinate with jars or boxes in which you keep dry cosmetic aids such as cotton wool for removing make-up.

Joss sticks and incense cones scent the air and add a certain mystical smokiness. You can buy joss-stick holders or trays that have small upright pillars into which the sticks can be slotted. Otherwise you can create your own with a bowl and some sand. The joss sticks will stick upright in the sand in the centre of the bowl and the ash will fall safely on the sand by the rim.

Many of the beautiful handmade soaps on the market are made with natural organic products such as oatmeal or herbs, which are sometimes suspended within the translucent bar. A few bars can be arranged in a bowl or glass jar and set on a sill by a window to make an attractive decorative feature.

Other washtime accessories include loofahs, real sponges, pumice stones and brushes to stimulate the circulation and remove dead skin. These natural products not only do their jobs extremely well but they also look attractive and can be arranged to dry on a decorative dish or bowl. Synthetic sponges tend to become slippery and smelly after a short time – something that will never happen to a natural sponge if it is left to dry thoroughly in an open space.

Loofahs make good back brushes and their rough texture has a slightly abrasive effect on the skin that can be useful for removing dead cells, leaving the skin fresh and revived. Pumice stone can help to reduce areas of hard skin that build up on the heels and soles of the feet

and the elbows. Oriental soaping brushes are useful for stirring up a soft sudsy lather in which to wash your face and body. The suds can be applied to the body in a circular motion to stimulate blood circulation.

Mirrors

Mirrors are an essential part of a bathroom, not only because they enable you to see yourself during the rituals of teeth-cleaning, shaving and applying make-up but also because they reflect light and make the room seem more airy and spacious than it is.

Among the most useful are non-mist mirrors, which do not steam up when the rest of the bathroom does. You can choose between those with a specially treated surface and those that are backed with a wafer-thin heating pad. The heated mirror has a minimal surface temperature and running costs are very low.

A bathroom may need two types of mirror: an ordinary one for general maintenance and a magnifying one for activities that involve close scrutiny. There are large normal mirrors that have a magnifying inset, and others in which a magnifying mirror is attached on an adjustable arm to the rim of a larger mirror. Some mirrors double as doors to cabinets and many are framed by the outer rim of the bathroom door. Mirror panels on sliding doors are also

Top right **Small magnifying mirrors are invaluable for close scrutiny. Some, such as the one shown here, are on a rigid wall mounts, but can be adjusted to achieve a better view.**
Centre right **This model has an extending arm with a magnifying mirror on one side and a normal mirror on the other.**
Bottom right **Another option is an extending mirror on a bi-fold arm – a model that is particularly easy to manipulate.**

available, and some cabinets have integral overhead lights so that the mirror is directly illuminated. A round or oval mirror makes an interesting alternative to the more traditional square mirror. A round mirror can be used to imitate a porthole in a bathroom with a nautical or submarine theme. Long vertical mirrors, usually found in the bedroom, can be desirable if the bathroom is also the place where you do exercises.

Shelves and racks

If you have plenty of wall space in the bathroom, try to place soap trays and shelves in close proximity to where they are needed. For example, an open-mesh wire-rimmed shelf is a practical accessory to have in a shower enclosure: the water can run through the open construction rather than leaving bars of soap melting in a puddle; the rim will prevent things from sliding off and ending up around your feet; and the shelf will hold shower gels, shampoos, conditioners and everything else you need in the appropriate place.

Open-mesh, wire-cornered shelves are also available, including sets of small shelves arranged in a vertical fashion that may be useful when installed above a bath. Recessed ceramic shelves may have an attractive appearance, but it can be difficult to reach objects set at the back

Opposite page, far left **A simple old wooden box can provide useful storage for dry items such as spare bars of soap, cotton buds and tissues.**

Opposite page, left **Soap can also be stored with linens,** such as towels and sheets; its perfume will permeate and freshen the linens.

Opposite page, below left **Bathroom scales are an indispensable accessory for those who like to keep track of their weight. A wicker** hamper is a convenient place to store spare towels or lavatory paper.

Below **Old jars from chemists, grocery stores or sweet shops can make attractive containers for bathroom products.**

of them, and they can become slimy and grubby with residue from soap and other lotions which accumulates and, when it is dried on, becomes hard to remove.

An old-fashioned accessory that survives because it does its job well is the classic bath rack. The open-mesh metal types allow water to drip off sponges, face cloths and soaps and back into the bath. The classic bath rack is a purely functional accessory but some versions have been modified to include a central section which tips up to support books, magazines and candle holders.

Glass shelves are often installed in front of the mirror and above the handbasin. They should be made of reinforced glass, either clear or opaque, and supported either by simple caps that slide over the ends of the glass or with metal rails that clip round the glass and hold it firm. The glass is likely to become marked with drips from bottles or tubes and will need regular cleaning.

A tooth mug attached to the wall and a soap dish either resting on the basin or attached to the wall help to keep some of the clutter off shelves. The tooth mug may be a glass, plastic or ceramic beaker held in a metal or plastic ring. The soap holder should be in a coordinated style. If you use liquid soap, you may be able to do without a soap tray. For solid soap, try to find a dish with a removable perforated tray that allows the excess water to drip away and lets the soap dry more quickly and efficiently. The water that collects in the under tray can then be easily thrown away.

Laundry baskets

A bathroom is the place where people commonly divest themselves of their dirty clothes, and a laundry basket is often found there. As well as its functional role, however, the basket or container for laundry can be an interesting decorative feature. Before buying such an accessory, decide how big you need it to be based on the volume of laundry that your household generates. If you take bed linen and bath towels directly to the washing machine, the basket in the bathroom need hold only small items. Also, if you use a dry cleaner or shirt-laundering service for large items of clothing, it will be needed simply for underwear and lightweight items such as T-shirts.

Laundry baskets come in many shapes and sizes. Choose one with a lid – to keep soiled clothes from view and also, especially if you do your laundry only once or twice a week, to contain any odours that may be emitted.

This page **Items frequently left out on a basin surround include soap and toothbrushes. Specifically designed toothbrush racks can be attached to the wall, but most people still seem to favour the tooth mug or beaker, which rests beside the basin and can be easily washed out when it becomes soiled.**

Lavatory seats and roll-holders

Most common designs of of lavatory seat are made from moulded plastic in a range of plain colours from which you can choose one that matches or complements the colour scheme of your room.

Victorian- and Edwardian-style bathrooms usually have wooden lavatory seats but these can also be found in modern bathrooms. Wood not only looks more attractive than plastic but also has the advantage of feeling warmer and more comfortable to sit on.

Make sure that any wooden lavatory seat you purchase is well sealed so that it can be effectively washed down from time to time with a mild detergent. Also available are jokey

Left and below **A toothbrush mug can be chosen to complement your bathroom scheme, but it should preferably be unbreakable like this opaque plastic one. Another container frequently found in the bathroom is the laundry basket, essential to hold used towels and items of clothing. The basket should have a lid to cover the contents and be waterproof to withstand the dampness of the bathroom as well as the moisture of the used towels. If your bathroom is small and you feel that a rigid container would take up too much space, a fabric laundry bag with a drawstring top can be hung behind the door.**

and decorative lavatory-seat covers made in transparent plastic into which seashells, sand, coins and any number of things have been arranged before the plastic has set. These can be amusing if you are following a flight-of-fancy decorative theme in your bathroom, or as a focus of interest in a small cloakroom.

Lavatory roll-holders are a functional necessity, but even here there are choices to be made. There is the basic plastic or wooden tube that runs through the centre of the roll and telescopes on a spring to allow the roll to be clipped in and out of the frame. Such holders are fiddly to use and the spring can become stretched or broken, which makes the whole mechanism inoperable.

The least complicated and most effective version is the metal cross bar. You simply slip the roll onto the bar and the slight return at the point keeps the roll in place. If you want to keep a few rolls to hand, store them in a small wicker basket or on a plain wooden pole on a base that stands on the floor and can be used to support a vertical stack of rolls.

Above and right **Plastic bins or baskets are available in many colours, and wood is a timeless classic which is suitable for the majority of decorative schemes.**

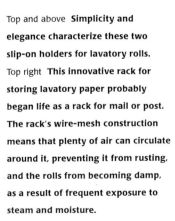

Top and above **Simplicity and elegance characterize these two slip-on holders for lavatory rolls.**

Top right **This innovative rack for storing lavatory paper probably began life as a rack for mail or post. The rack's wire-mesh construction means that plenty of air can circulate around it, preventing it from rusting, and the rolls from becoming damp, as a result of frequent exposure to steam and moisture.**

Right **Traditional and contemporary wall-mounted bar towel rails flank a more decorative towel ring.**

Towels and mats

Towels can be regarded as an accessory in a bathroom. Neatly stacked and folded, they can bring colour and texture to a room as well as being inviting to wrap yourself up in.

There are a number of types and textures of towels, ranging from the coarser linen and natural cotton types, which are invigorating after a morning shower and absorbent and light next to the skin, to the velvet-pile towels, which are thick and plush, and envelope and absorb water rather than stimulate the skin. The choice of colour is almost limitless, but if you like white towels, which feel the cleanest and look wonderful in a generous stack, ensure that they stay white rather than absorbing various shades of pink and grey from being mistakenly put in a coloured wash.

Towelling is often used for bathmats, which are generally chosen to co-ordinate with bath and hand towels. Cork mats are also good, especially when you step out of the shower, and they feel soft and warm underfoot. Cork mats should be pre-treated so that they are water-resilient rather than absorbent. Another option is duckboard, which should be placed on a tiled or linoleum-covered floor because water will run straight off the body, through the open wooden framework and onto the floor.

The Japanese taoru wash cloth is a skimpy towel for mopping the brow; it is also rolled up and used for scrubbing the body, then unfurled, rinsed and squeezed so that it can help to mop off surplus water after bathing. The equivalent in the West would be a face cloth, but our more familiar little towelling squares are not substantial enough to cope with all these demands.

Towel rails

Unheated towel rails are available in wood, plastic or metal in the form of a ring or a straightforward bar held in place by two brackets. These towel rails can be attached to a wall beside the basin or on the front or side of a cabinet. The rail allows the towel to dry more efficiently after use because it has space for the towel to be spread out; in a ring the material of the towel is restricted and folds over on itself time and again, which means that it stays damper for longer.

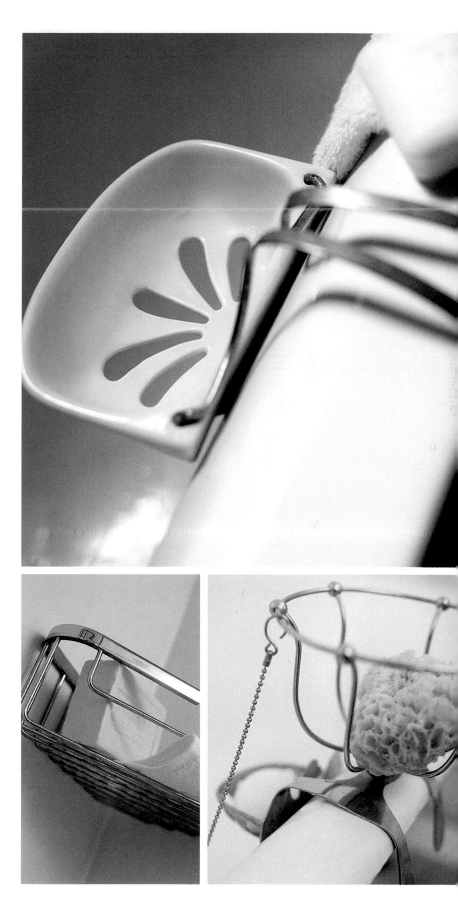

Top right **This soap dish hangs over the side of the bath, remaining attached by means of a simple arched metal bracket. Its perforations resemble stylized flower petals. To permit water to drain away easily from the wet soap, soap dishes need to have a perforated base. If the dish has no water outlet, the wet soap will melt and form a slimy residue in the base.**

Right **This shelf tray is ideal for a shower enclosure. It has been fixed into the corner of two tiled walls and any water from the shower or soap will pass straight through.**
Far right **This stylish holder has substantial gaps between the metal supports so is more useful for holding large items such as sponges, loofahs and face cloths rather than slippery bars of soap.**

4
surfaces and decoration

walls and surrounds

flooring

colour

display

THE POPULARITY OF CLASSIC WHITE FIXTURES MEANS THAT THE CHARACTER OF A BATHROOM IS USUALLY DEFINED BY THE DECORATION, FLOORING AND FINISHES TO WALLS AND OTHER SURFACES. THE GROUNDWORK IS EXTREMELY IMPORTANT. PLASTER WALLS SHOULD BE CLEANED, PREPARED, FILLED AND SANDED TO THE HIGHEST STANDARDS, AND TREATED AND UNDERCOATED SO THAT THE SURFACES ARE SEALED AND SMOOTH BEFORE PAPER, PAINT OR TILES ARE APPLIED.

Any chip, crack or area of peeling paint will become rapidly worse with repeated exposure to the damp and steamy atmosphere of a bathroom. For safety's sake it is important that surfaces, especially the floor, should be smooth – uneven tiles may cause you to stub your toe or slip, which could be dangerous. Furthermore, the surfaces that come into immediate contact with the body are more comfortable if they are smooth and soft rather than roughly textured.

Bathrooms are often small rooms; sometimes they have no windows or only a small window. In these situations you need to create the impression of space. This can be done by using pale colours and by keeping pattern to a minimum – an abundance of pattern can make the space seem small and crowded. Conversely, in a large bathroom you may decide to use darker colours to make the room seem more intimate. Adding patterned tile borders or surrounds will also help to break up large plain areas.

Paint is one of the most durable decorative finishes in a bathroom, and there are many types of paint specially formulated for the bathroom atmosphere. But painted walls don't have to be plain – although marbling, dragging and sponging paint effects are now rather dated, there are plenty of other unusual and stimulating schemes that can be used to bring an unexpected element to bathroom walls. Murals

can be effective and may vary from extravagant, such as the view of an ancient Greek ruin or temple, to thematic, such as an underwater water lagoon scene complete with coral and fishes. A trompe l'oeil view through a fake window brings a touch of outdoors inside. Even a simple graded-colour effect may be interesting: you can start with the darkest colour at the bottom and build up to the lightest near the ceiling, or vice versa – an effect that can also be achieved with ceramic tiles.

Ceramic tiles have long been a standard part of the decorative armoury, but developments in the use of materials are opening up new alternatives. Glass, steel, stone and wood are all now not only acceptable but also desirable. They can be made part of an exciting and unusual scheme for one of the most intimate and indulgent rooms in the house.

You also need to decide what type of flooring to install and to choose the edging and surrounds for the bath and basin. When investigating the range of the surfaces on the market, try to keep practicality in mind. A rough, dark grey slate may have initial appeal, but think of the difficulty of removing spots of dried toothpaste from the crevices and stray hairs from between the ridges. Smooth surfaces are in general the simplest to wipe down and keep clean and hygienic.

walls and surrounds

Bathroom surfaces should be water-resistant and smooth to the touch. Traditionally, the areas that came into most regular contact with water were tiled and the rest of the room was either coated with paint or hung with vinyl-treated wallpaper. Paint is still popular, but the paint finishes and the variety and sizes of ceramic tiles are changing to keep up with developments in contemporary design.

Some bathrooms are decorated with wallpaper, but the textured vinyl finishes of the 1970s and 1980s have been overtaken by more subtle stripes and toile de Jouy patterns. Wallpapers are best used in areas away from the main sources of water and steam. They are also suitable for upper parts of the room, such as the wall space above a band of tiles or around the doorway and window, where more air circulates. A small bathroom, in which the area available for papering is limited, may be the place where the more colourful or expensive designs are hung, because the impact or cost is restricted by the small amount that can be used.

As well as the traditional surface coverings, many new materials can be seen in the bathroom. Glass, plaster, stone and wood are popular in modern schemes. These organic surfaces work well with traditional white fixtures and with hard steel finishes – the tactile and earthy finishes of the plaster and stone soften the sometimes aggressive lines of the steel.

Ordinary plaster is not generally suitable for bathrooms unless it is carefully finished with a waterproof seal – otherwise the plaster will absorb water and eventually start to powder and shale. Any cracks, even in waterproofed plaster, can absorb moisture and become damaged. Types of plaster that can withstand the rigours of the bathroom include Armourcast, which contains a durable marble dust. Walls and surfaces to which plaster is applied should be well prepared, and the finished dry wall should be waxed, varnished or sealed.

Laminated surfaces should be used sparingly and carefully in bathrooms to avoid the 'fitted kitchen' look. Some of the strong single-coloured finishes are bright and contemporary and can be pre-formed with smooth curves and soft edges into individual, freestanding pieces of furniture.

Where possible, the corners of surrounds, cabinets, cupboards and units should be rounded or capped so that they are not likely to cause injury. When you are planning which materials to put where, remember that cold surfaces such as tiles are best kept at a distance – behind a handbasin or on the far side of the bath – so that, when you are naked, relaxed and warm from your shower or bath, you won't brush up against or lean on anything that will be cold enough to give you a shock.

Glass

Glass is durable and easy to clean. It can be plain or opaque, coloured or clear, but it should be used in a bathroom only if it has been laminated or toughened. Lamination involves sandwiching liquid resin between two sheets of glass. If one sheet of the laminated glass breaks, the other remains intact, and most of the shattered glass remains attached to the sheet by virtue of the laminate to which it is stuck.

Toughened glass is heat-treated to make it four times more durable than standard glass. If and when toughened glass breaks, it crumbles into small lumps rather than sharp shards. In some modern schemes, safety glass – which is reinforced by fine lines of wire running through it in a grid pattern – has also been used for bathroom surfaces. This glass has a slight blue/green cast and sometimes comes with a textured finish. Shower enclosures are often made of toughened glass; it can

Left **Toughened glass is not only smooth and easy to clean but it also has a visual affinity with water. It can be cut and used as a surround for a basin or as a splashback.**
Top and above **Heavy-duty materials such as stone and marble give solidity and opulence to a scheme and can provide an interesting contrast to plain white ceramic and enamelled bathroom fixtures.**

also be used to create surfaces around handbasins and splashbacks around the edges of bathtubs. One advantage of a glass splashback is that any pattern or design that appears on the wall behind it will show through, so that a wallpaper or a collage of cuttings will be protected but still visible.

Glass is not in itself an expensive material but the process of having it cut to size, finished and erected can be costly. The glass sheets or walls need to be cut to the exact size and the edges polished or rounded off-site, then all the items have to be transported to their destination and assembled. When the glass is in place and secured, the edges and joins, especially in shower enclosures, must be carefully sealed.

Above **This textural finish has been applied over the walls and outer surfaces of the bath, making it look as though it has been hewn from a piece of rock.**

Top right **Stone can be used in many ways. Fine sheets can be applied as façades or panels, and larger blocks or slabs used to form basins and baths.**

Stone

Stone has good waterproof qualities and comes in many types and finishes. Marble, once found only in rich households, is now more widely and cheaply available in tiles, veneers and marble and resin composites. The composites are invariably lighter than the pure stone and can have a warmer, slightly softer touch. They are also easier to cut and can be pre-moulded into a number of shapes.

Limestone and granite both come in a range of muted natural colours, and can be bought in tile form as well as cut to order for a splashback or sink area. The advantage of specially cut lengths is that there are no joins or gaps that need to be sealed to prevent water dripping through. The drawback of a stone surface is that any glass or china that is accidentally dropped on it will almost certainly crack or break, and if you knock against it with bare skin you may suffer bruising.

Wood and fibreboard

Like plaster, wood provides an attractive soft finish in a bathroom but it should be carefully selected for its water resilience and protectively treated. Constant contact with water can cause kiln-dried and naturally dried wood to split, and the water may stain and mark an unfinished or a natural surface. Although there are many paler woods available, the current fashion is for dark wood. Teak is an endangered species, but rubberwood, iorko and merbau are acceptable substitutes. Many tropical woods have inherent water-repellent and anti-bacterial properties.

Wood is generally best kept at a distance from detergents, especially those containing bleach. Wood soaps are useful for cleaning; alternatively, a clean damp cloth will remove surface build-up. For woods that lack good water tolerance it is necessary to seal the surfaces exposed to water with a polyurethane finish, yacht varnish or one recommended by the timber yard or carpenter.

Another popular surface for bathroom walls and cupboards is tongue and groove timber panelling. This type of finish – which can be painted, or left plain and sealed to achieve one of a variety of looks – creates a homely environment. Tongue and groove, also known as T&G, can be used to conceal unsightly items, from uneven walls to ugly pipework and lavatory cisterns. If the bathroom is large, cladding the walls below dado height with tongue and groove panelling will make it seem smaller and cosier.

Another material suitable for surface building in a bathroom is medium density fibreboard, known as MDF. This can be routed to create panel-like sections similar to tongue and groove or recessed panels. You can buy or make fancy edging strips with MDF – in scalloped shapes, for example – to bring pattern and a decorative finish to a frieze, the top of a cupboard or the edge of a bath panel. MDF must be well sealed and finished.

Metal

Sheets of steel can be lightweight, water-resistant and moulded to form a seamless basin and splashback in one. Bath panels and surrounds can also be pre-formed. But too much steel can make a bathroom appear cold and inhospitable; it should be mixed with natural materials and softened by the use of colour, either on the walls or in accessories such as towels. Steel should be cleaned with a soft cloth and an abrasive-free cream or aerosol product. Small bits of grit or wire can mark the surface and change a gleaming smooth finish into a maze of tiny scratches that will eventually create a dull, worn appearance.

Paint

Most leading paint manufacturers now make ranges of paint suitable for bathrooms, including vinyl matt, vinyl silk and vinyl soft sheen. Surfaces that are covered with vinyl paints are easy to wipe clean with a cloth and a mild detergent. An anti-condensation

Above right **Shades of white and soft sandstone are combined in a scheme that is clean but warm. Painted surfaces are available in myriad colours as well as in a number of vinyl and waterproof finishes. Varying the size of tiles can introduce pattern. For example, you could place large tiles on the floor and smaller, patchwork-like ones of the same colour on the walls. The variety in size creates a variety of focus.**
Right **The panelling of the cupboards in the foreground and units beyond echoes the chequerboard design formed by the tiles on the floor and wall and in the bath panel.**

Left **The reflective quality of the mirror on the cabinet and splashback contrasts well with the solid, matt appearance of the sink and wall surface.**
Bottom left **The jigsaw-like quality of this wood panelling adds interest and colour to the room.**

The grain of the wood runs in different directions and the panels are in a variety of sizes.
Below **A crazy paving of stone flags creates a rough interior to this shower. The various shades of the stone and the haphazard shapes add to its appeal.**

paint is available that reduces build-up of condensation and contains a fungicide to protect the surface against mould growth. This sort of paint is ideal for use around a shower enclosure with an open top, where steam rises and cools, covering the wall with rivulets of moisture.

As in any other room, the surfaces to be painted must be carefully prepared to achieve a smooth finish, but where there will be an abundance of steam and condensation, especially around the sink, shower and bath areas, the preparation should be carried out with extra care. Any cracks, chips or uneven patches may lead to the paint lifting or chipping – a problem aggravated by hot, damp conditions. There are many finishes that can be achieved with paint, but in a bathroom, where wallpaper borders and friezes are vulnerable to peeling and damage, painted stencil patterns can be a good alternative. Many companies make stencil kits with pre-cut shapes and a selection of brushes and sponges with which to apply the paint. The stencils can be applied in a band around the top of the ceiling, as a dado rail, or even in a line above the skirting board. But avoid using them in all three places. Be sparing with this type of decoration – otherwise it becomes intrusive and messy.

Tiles

Ceramic tiles have long been a standard wall covering for bathrooms. Particularly popular today are the small mosaic tiles that come in strips with removable backing for easy positioning and fixing. The mesh or brown paper backing can simply be cut with a pair of scissors or a sharp knife and the unwanted section of tiles put to one side for later use. Attached to the upper surface of the tiles, the mesh also ensures that the strips of tiles are placed at regular distances apart. Once the reverse side of the tiles have been laid and cemented in place, the mesh is removed.

Mosaic tiles can be used to create many different patterns or pictures. Some images, like those seen on the floors of the sites of ancient Romans baths, are of gods and emperors; others are simple bands of geometric pattern. Another interesting effect can be achieved by starting with a very pale shade at the bottom of the wall and building up to a deep intense shade of the same colour at the top. This can be achieved in regular bands of colour or in a random, wavelike pattern.

If you are laying standard-sized tiles (100 x 100 millimetres), try making a pattern with plain tiles rather than using surface-patterned or transfer-decorated tiles. For example, the square tiles can be placed on their points to form diamonds. Oblong, brick-shaped tiles can be set in regular lines or

staggered so that they overlap. Mixing shapes and colours can also be interesting. A simple chequerboard effect can be produced with the traditional black and white tiles or with light and dark shades of the same colour. If placed at the top and bottom of a wall of square tiles, lines of oblong tiles can be used to give the impression of a dado and skirting board; a similar arrangement of diamond and square tiles in two or three shades of the same colour can also create an unusual and attractive effect.

As an alternative to the traditional factory-made glazed ceramic tiles, there are unique hand-made and painted designs. Some of these have objects or pieces of metal pressed into them. Glass tiles are also available in a rainbow of colours.

Matt effects include encaustic tiles, where the pattern is made from inlaying contrasting colours of clay in the surface of the tile. This style of decoration was first used in medieval church and monastery flooring but has been updated to provide innovative designs with natural, non-gloss, stone-like finishes.

Opposite page, far left **If you have large windows and good access to natural light, dark surfaces can be interesting, but they may be claustrophobic in a small, badly lit room.**

Opposite page, top left **Carrying the mosaic theme through from the floor to the lower half of the wall and the bath surround creates a dividing line between the upper, clear part of the room and the lower area, where the fixtures are plumbed in.**

Opposite page, below left, and this page, left and above **If grouting between tiles discolours with age and wear, it can be cleaned or replaced. An alternative is to tint the grout before you apply it so that it reflects the colour of the tiles. This will make it less obvious than white and less likely to show stains and marks.**

Ceramic tiles are still one of the most widely used surfaces in bathrooms. They come in a variety of shapes and sizes and in an infinite range of colours. Although the shiny glazed finish has been dominant for some time, matt finishes are becoming more popular – many have an earthy, organic, stone-like quality that appeals to contemporary designers.

Right These plain oblong tiles, reminiscent of bricks, have a 1930s feel. They may also recall hospitals and other clinical environments, so they should be used with care and teamed with accessories that soften the utilitarian effect.

Below This multicoloured panel and splashback also uses brick-style tiles but the strong colours banish any clinical overtones and the shape of the tiles echoes that of the red bricks used in the adjacent wall.

Below right Small tiles are easier than large ones to apply to curved surfaces.

Opposite page, top A band of tiles, the same size and colour as those used on the wall, has been used to create a border beneath the rim of the bath.

Opposite page, far right Special edging strips can be used to seal and get round corners where cutting and butting up individual tiles is too difficult.

If your bathroom tiles are in good condition but the wrong colour, or if you just want to give the place a new look, use a preparation formulated to cope with tile surfaces. Ordinary emulsion is hard to apply to the shining glass finish and, even when dry, will easily scratch off or peel.

Existing tiles can be painted over and given a new look with specially devised primers and paints. The primer is a base coat which creates a surface to which the paint can adhere. Once dry, the scratch-resistant top coat can then be applied. There are also paints that will cover melamine surfaces, which have a similar shiny finish to tiles. You can update marble-effect or patterned melamine by painting it in a plain strong colour. Again, a primer must be applied to a clean, dry, dust-free surface. The top coat may be applied when the primer is dry.

The grouting between tiles is an area where grime can gather and discolour the joins. This is particularly noticeable when white or pale-coloured tiles have been used. Rather than raking out the existing grout and re-doing it, you could try a specialist device such as a grout pen. This is an applicator containing a paint-based solution that can be easily and simply drawn over the grouting to refresh and brighten it.

When you need to apply grout, choose classic white, which looks clean and fresh. Grey grout can seem dirty next to pale colours, and strongly coloured grouts date quickly. White is also less intrusive and ensures that the tile has more decorative prominence than the utilitarian filler.

Flooring should be durable, waterproof and non-slip. In many simply furnished and unadorned modern bathrooms, the flooring has also become the focus of colour and decoration. Lighter shades help a small space to appear larger, and a dark colour makes a large space look warmer and more intimate.

flooring

Bathroom flooring must be able to withstand repeated exposure to water and steam. Joins in coverings such as linoleum should be kept to a minimum and away from the centre of the room. If possible, lay the flooring before the bath is installed – if you have a rolltop with claw feet, for example, you will be able to see under the bath, where the flow of the floor covering should be uninterrupted.

Many bathrooms are small rooms, so a single colour on the floor will give an impression of space; a heavily patterned linoleum or vinyl-tile design will be too busy and overpowering. The main problem with dark flooring in a bathroom is that it shows up dust, talcum powder and pale-coloured hairs which are not so visible on the

lighter coverings. When selecting a floor covering, think of comfort, safety and hygiene as well as colour and pattern. It is worth visiting builders' merchants and commercial flooring outlets as well as the usual domestic retailers so that you are aware of all the options. Carpet is one possibility, but cork, wood, rubber, linoleum and vinyl flooring are much better options because they are easy to clean as well as being comfortable under bare feet.

Carpet and matting

Although carpet has sometimes been fashionable as a bathroom floor covering, providing a feeling of luxury and softness underfoot, it is generally best avoided. If you want to put carpet in a bathroom, chose a variety that is rubber-backed and preferably wool or other natural fibre rather than synthetic. Acrylic and nylon stain easily unless pre-protected with a stain-resistant finish. They can also generate a lot of static electricity. If carpet is laid in a large, well-ventilated room, any build-up of moisture and dampness will evaporate quickly. However, if a carpet is to be laid in a small bathroom, you need to install an extractor fan or some form of ventilation – otherwise mould may form and the carpet backing will start to rot.

Carpet is difficult to clean thoroughly. Hairs, nail clippings and sloughed-off skin may become entangled in the pile and any spilt bath product, oil or nail varnish is

Far left **The square insets in this diamond-patterned tiled floor lift the simple layout and add another colour.**
Left **This wooden floor has a warm colouring but is pale**

and reflective, giving an overall light appearance.
Above **Wooden floors must be well sealed or finished to avoid splinters and to make them water-resistant.**

quickly absorbed, leaving a stain. Certain areas such as those around the lavatory can become marked and odorous. Natural matting materials, such as coir, sisal and jute, have similar disadvantages to carpet, and some are vulnerable to water damage. The rougher textured finishes feel prickly underfoot.

Mats and rugs are popular in bathrooms, especially where the flooring is hard and cold. Mats must be carefully positioned and, for safety, should be held in place with rubber backing or carpet grip. The best mats for bathrooms are made from absorbent materials such as towelling or cotton. These not only soak up water that drips from the body and feet after showering or bathing but also can be regularly put into the washing machine and thoroughly cleaned.

Cork

Cork comes from the outer bark of the cork oak, *Quercus suber*, and has the advantage of being a renewable resource because the tree replaces the bark it loses. Cork is a good insulator against cold and noise and has a soft cushion-like feel underfoot; it is durable and, if sealed, resilient to wear and tear.

The natural colour of cork is a warm honey-brown. It can be stained or coloured in many shades, but it should always be sealed with a polyurethane finish.

Buy cork that has already been impregnated rather than trying to add the sealant once the floor is in place. Flooring that is insufficiently sealed may swell and crack if it absorbs water from a spill or flood.

Cork can be bought in tiles or by the roll. There are various grades of thickness, so make sure that you choose the sort that is suitable for floors rather than the thinner product intended for walls. Some tiles are not only impregnated with a water-repellent finish but also have a solid rubber backing, which makes them ideal for the bathroom and increases warmth and sound insulation.

Wood

Bare wood is not an ideal bathroom floor covering because it can be damaged by water and extremes of temperature, but if the wood is treated, seasoned and sealed it can provide a natural and versatile surface. The colour of a wooden floor varies according to the type of tree it comes from. Expensive hardwoods such as elm, ash, walnut, oak and maple are best left in their natural colour so that their intrinsic beauty and the pattern of the grain will show through.

Cheaper softwoods such as pine can be decorated with paint washes and stains – a technique that may also be used to revive damaged or time-worn wooden

Below **The area around the lavatory should have an easy-to-clean surface, such as this decking, which can be washed with hot water.**
Right **Wood intended for use in a bathroom, especially on a surface that will often be wet, needs to be specially prepared and finished.**

Right **Wooden decking is warm underfoot and can be laid over a floor made of stone or a similar cold material. In this bathroom there is a stone floor in the shower, which is warmed by cascades of hot water. However, the floor outside, where the bather stands to get dry, is made of wood, making it comfortable to touch with bare feet. The floor area in front of the basin is also made of stone, but someone standing there is more likely to be dry and wearing slippers.**

Below **Rubber matting used to be confined to public thoroughfares and industrial sites but is now commonly seen in domestic bathrooms. It is hard-wearing and water-resistant.**

Right **Stone floors need to be very carefully laid. The cutting, especially in corners, should be accurately done, and the joins should be small, neat and regular. The gaps between the stone slabs must be sealed to prevent water from seeping under them and rotting the boards or wooden joists beneath.**

floors. To create an all-over pale-lime effect, apply a wash of white paint diluted with white spirit or water to a clean floor surface with a wide brush or sponge. Apply one coat at a time and leave it to dry thoroughly so that you can assess the depth of colour before applying any additional coats. It is easier to put on two or three coats to build up the strength of a colour than to reduce the intensity of a colour as it is soaking into the surface of the wood. With a limed finish the grain of the wood should be clearly visible; the aim is to convey a hint of colour rather than a slab of solid paint.

By using two or three colours of wash you can create a chequerboard effect on the floor. As well as diluted paints, stronger and richer shades can be achieved with specific wood stains and dyes. Stencil patterns can also be used to add border interest, but allow the base colour to dry thoroughly before applying the next or adjacent colour – otherwise the two colours may bleed and run into each other.

Limed, stained and painted floors should all be finished with a water-resistant sealant such as gloss or matt varnish. For a really durable finish, choose marine varnish – used to seal the wooden decks of boats – but you may need to apply several coats to build up a waterproof seal. Marine varnish takes a long time to dry, as does the more usual polyurethane varnish. But doing the job properly will result in a long-lasting and hard-wearing finish. Existing wooden floors can also be sanded and painted, but make sure that you seal them again with several coats of varnish or recommended finish.

Wooden floors come in a variety of shapes and styles, from planks to parquet. If you are planning to lay a new wooden floor, ask the supplier which type is best for your circumstances, taking into account not only cost but also the size and character of the room. By laying planks parallel to the length of the room you can make it appear longer;

Right If you are installing a bath on legs, lay the floor first and then put the bath on top to avoid the problem of having to tile around the legs. If the side of the bath is destined to be panelled, the flooring can be laid up to the edge of the bath and the panel placed over it for a neat join.

Above right **Water sprays in all directions in an open shower room, so the walls and floor are not the only areas that need to be sealed.**

Far right **The corner is where many tiles meet; water may also cascade down the walls at that point, building up a small reservoir.**

if you lay the planks across the width, the room will seem wider. Another interesting way to achieve a pattern with a plain wooden floor is to lay the planks in a line from the corner of the room so that they are diagonal to the walls.

Ask the timber or varnish supplier about the best way to maintain and clean the surface of the floor. Wooden floors are easy to sweep clean and can be mopped with a damp sponge, but some finishes should be cleaned only with a particular recommended product rather than a harsh detergent or bleach, which may cause damage.

Rubber, linoleum and vinyl

Rubber flooring has traditionally been used for industrial coverings in warehouses, store rooms and commercial kitchens. Most rubber flooring is textured with a raised pattern or ribbing which creates a non-slip surface.

Available in sheet or tile form, and in a wide range of colours and finishes, rubber is attached with a strong adhesive to a solid base. If you want to lay it on an existing floor of wooden planks, you may first have to lay a subfloor of wooden sheeting or MDF so that the floor

Left **The mosaic theme seen in the border around the wall has been borrowed to make a small, mat-like pattern on the floor.**
Above **Laying diamonds of contrasting colour is a subtle but interesting way to break up a plain floor.**
Top right **Dark-coloured mosaic wall and floor tiles have been used to give a sense of depth and unity.**
Right **Before laying small tiles it is crucial that the ground work is well done. If the tiles are laid on floorboards that move, or on an uneven surface, they will lift and crack. Broken tiles both look untidy and are potentially dangerous.**
Far right **Black and white chequerboard tiles are a classic floor covering that suits simple schemes in both contemporary and traditional styles.**

Hard flooring

The varieties of hard flooring used in modern designs include concrete, slate, stone, terracotta and ceramic tiles. Many of these finishes have traditionally been disregarded as bathroom flooring because they are cold underfoot, but the recent vogue for underfloor heating – enjoyed by the ancient Romans – has meant that an ever increasing number of people are turning to these materials for water-resilient, hardwearing finishes.

Concrete can be laid in a thin screed onto a sealed subfloor and the heating conduits laid in place and smoothed over before the concrete sets. The surface of the concrete can be finished to create a smooth, slightly shiny appearance or lightly textured with a wood-grain effect or simple linear marks. Alternatively, it can be coloured with dyeing agents to give a warmer and more domestic appearance or – for something more unusual and exciting – powdered resins can be added to the concrete to give a sparkle and lustre to what is often regarded as a dull material.

Concrete is durable, waterproof and easy to clean, but anything fragile that is dropped on it will almost certainly break. The plain appearance of a standard concrete floor can be broken up with mats, rugs or small sections of wooden duckboard placed in appropriate areas of the floor.

Slate – another natural material that has been shunned as flooring for some time – is now enjoying something of a revival. It too has benefited from underfloor heating, and from modern finishes that make it more resilient and less likely to shale or flake. Slate is waterproof and comes in beautiful earthy tones ranging from green and blue-grey to amber pink. The main disadvantage of a slate floor is that it can be noisy when metal or furniture or accessories are dragged or moved over it. Other stone floor coverings such as granite are similarly hard and noisy but they are also hardwearing and waterproof, and come in a whole spectrum of colours

surface is stable and will not cause the tiles to move and tear over joins. Rubber flooring has a certain amount of sound insulation; it is also water-resistant and can be cleaned thoroughly with a brush or a mop.

Used as a floor covering for more than a century, linoleum is made from a combination of natural ingredients – linseed oil, finely ground wood, pine resin and natural pigments – pressed onto a jute backing. A reasonably flexible product, it is strong, easy to clean, water-resistant and comparatively warm underfoot. If you have a linoleum floor, be careful to prevent water from seeping under the joins or edges because this may cause the jute to absorb the water and lift the linoleum off the floor.

Vinyl is a chemically manufactured covering available in many colours and patterns. As is the case with certain linoleum products, vinyl flooring can be laser-cut to order to create a wide range of patterns and pictures. Pre-cut patterns and insets are also available. Vinyl comes in a variety of thicknesses and finishes and some, such as cushioned vinyl, are ideal for the bathroom because they have a soft and spongy feel underfoot.

Although tiles of rubber, linoleum and vinyl can be laid by a competent DIY person, sheets or rolls of these materials may be unwieldy and difficult to manoeuvre in a confined space. To avoid making a crucial error when cutting and laying a single area of flooring, it is probably worth paying a little extra to have the floor laid by a professional.

If you decide to do it yourself, make an accurate paper template of the floor, including all the tricky areas, such as those around the pedestals of the lavatory and handbasin. Lay the material flat in a garden or larger room, then use the template to cut out precisely the shape of the area that you need to cover.

from white to black, with flecks of gold- and silver-coloured metals in their seams which give an appearance of luxury. These surfaces are good in a bathroom with a steam cabinet because they will not be badly affected by high temperatures or a damp atmosphere.

Tiles made of materials such as terracotta and ceramic are durable, waterproof and less expensive than those made of stone or slate. Terracotta tiles can be manufactured with a textured and handmade appearance. The slight roughness of the surface is not unpleasant underfoot and creates a certain level of non-slip safety. Ceramic tiles used on the floor should be of the sort that have been specially made for the purpose rather than those meant for use on walls or work surfaces, and they may be more satisfactory with a matt rather than a shiny finish. Shiny tiles can become slippery when wet, creating a source of potential danger.

Although usually used in walls or to build semi-opaque panels, glass bricks can also be inset into a floor. In an area overlooking a stairwell or an extension cantilevered over a lower floor, glass bricks can be used to give a light and airy appearance. They are especially effective in an otherwise windowless room.

Mosaic is another water-resistant and decorative floor covering. Again, it was the ancient Romans who pioneered the use of mosaic tiles, to adorn the interiors of their bath houses. Mosaics can be made from stone – even from pebbles, although they tend

Left **A classic mosaic pattern, modelled on those found in Roman bath houses or villas, uses the colours that have been chosen for the paint work and marble surround of the bath. The floor is the only source of pattern in an otherwise plain scheme.**
Above **A detail of the mosaic floor shows how the tiny sections form a pattern in addition to the pattern created by the coloured design.**
Right **In a more modern interpretation of mosaic, the floor and wall have been covered with oblong sections of tile in a variety of shades of the same colour and cut in a variety of widths.**

to be knobbly to walk on – and glazed matt or vitreous glass tiles. Laying a mosaic picture requires skill and patience. The design must be accurately assembled on the floor, in a dry state, before being set into cement.

If the idea of laying a whole picture strikes you as too daunting, then a small frieze or border, or simply the immediate area under the shower in a wet room, can be decorated to interesting effect.

If you are planning to use any of the heavy hard-floor surfaces, such as stone, marble or even ceramic tiles, on an upper or

suspended floor, seek the advice of a surveyor or an architect before you go ahead. With expert help, you need to calculate the total weight of the flooring plus a bathful of water and work out if the existing beams are capable of supporting the load without special reinforcement.

colour

Colour is a very personal thing. Different people respond and react differently to various depths and tones of colour, so your choice of decoration must be determined by your own taste or as a joint decision or compromise with your partner or family.

The best way to test a colour is to apply a good-sized patch of paint, around a metre square, to a wall and live with it for a few days. Walk past it in the morning, look at it in subdued light at night and in full sunlight at midday. If you can get matchpot testers in several shades, paint patches in various parts of the room so that you can compare them at the same times of day.

Yellows, oranges and reds

Some people believe that colour can affect your frame of mind and be used to enhance certain moods and periods of relaxation. For example, yellow is a sunny colour and – said to be the first colour that the human eye registers – it is also believed to lift the spirits. Yellow tones can vary from the merest hint, which simply warms up a white paint, to the powerful impact of a vivid

buttercup shade. When choosing a shade of yellow for your bathroom, try it out in different lights. The intensity of colour will vary depending on whether it is seen in daylight or in the glow of artificial light. The change can be quite dramatic – from a medium tone of lively yellow to a rich and opulent golden hue.

Orange is a colour that most people either love or hate. It is believed to stimulate the appetite and bring a feeling of warmth – but people with fiery tempers are often advised to avoid living in an environment with too much orange. It is also a fashionable colour that may date quickly.

A strong colour like orange should be used in moderation in a bathroom. Instead of painting all the walls bright orange, you could paint one or more of the walls in a more muted shade. You could also use a small

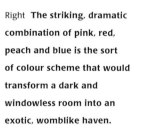

Right **The striking, dramatic combination of pink, red, peach and blue is the sort of colour scheme that would transform a dark and windowless room into an exotic, womblike haven.**

Opposite page **This gold and orange crackle-glaze wall has an opulent, luxurious feel. The fragmented effect of the paint finish also complements the marble pillar and the old stone basin. The gold and orange are a warm, rich combination that can** add to the enjoyment of a relaxing and indulgent soak in the bath.
Left **The decorative floor and the large framed painting bring together the white and all the earthy tones that have been used elsewhere in the scheme.**

connotations, but some people regard it a cold colour whereas others find it relaxing and tranquil. Some shades of blue have been 'hotted' up with a hint of red or yellow making them slightly purple or green. Turquoise, a mixture of blue and green, is a fresh zingy shade but, like purple, it has a tendency to go in and out of fashion, which may mean that a room painted in this colour will quickly look dated.

Green is a healing colour reminiscent of nature, growth and rebirth. It can bring a freshness and liveliness to a bathroom in the morning, especially the paler shades such as almond, mint or apple; but stronger shades such as emerald or malachite look rich and luxurious in subdued lighting – which makes green a colour worth considering for a single bathroom that needs to cater for these two moods.

White and cream, brown and black

White, a colour associated with purity and spirituality, has long been a favourite in bathrooms – not just for fixtures, but for tiles and paint as well. It provides a neutral background against which coloured accessories and decorative items can be placed. It also gives a feeling of freshness and cleanliness. However, too much white can create an atmosphere that is cold and austere, and marks on white paint are instantly noticeable.

Cream and off-white shades combine the clean appearance of white with enough warmth to soften a potentially clinical environment. There has been a trend among paint companies to use primary colours as a base to produce slightly coloured whites that are described as, for example, a 'hint' of blue or a 'hint' of yellow.

Brown is rarely found in bathroom paint or tiles, but in the 1960s and 1970s there was a vogue for chocolate brown and the wheat-coloured pampas acrylic bathware. Brown is an earthy colour with connotations of soil and bark – thought of as dirty and rough, and therefore incompatible with the cleansing activities that occur in a bathroom – but shades of brown appear in wood, which is popular as a decorative surface.

Black may be overpowering if it appears on all four walls, but it can be used to frame a feature or panels, and in borders. Black accessories can also be dramatic against a pale-coloured background and when used in tiles combined in a chequerboard effect with contrasting colours such as

amount of a stronger shade in painting the area around a large mirror or window in the form of a frame, making it a secondary element rather than a primary one. Like orange, red – said to signify danger, dominance and decadence – can be overpowering, especially in a small room. Vivid vermilion can be startling and is best used in moderation, but red mixed with a touch of blue becomes a rich and restful burgundy. Darker shades of red may make a large bathroom feel smaller and more intimate, but it will not create an invigorating place to wash in the morning unless you add plenty of glass, mirror and chrome to lighten up the overall scheme.

Pinks, purples, blues and greens

Pink can be a calming and relaxing colour, although the more modern shade of shocking pink is lively and energetic. Shades of pink can give a bathroom a delicate and feminine feel and, because it is at the paler end of the spectrum, pale pink harmonizes well with classic white fixtures.

Purple comes in and out of vogue. Paler shades such as lavender and lilac can, like pink, work well with white fixtures and silver or chrome accessories. Deeper shades of purple make a space feel smaller, and a very dark shade may be oppressive. All sorts of blues are popular in bathrooms – from the palest wash of sky blue to a deep rich navy. Blue has watery

cream or pink. Shiny black surfaces can be difficult to keep clean – soap marks and toothpaste smears have a tendency to show up as white scum or rings, so black tiles and glazed surfaces are not advisable for shower walls or around the handbasin, unless you are prepared to wipe and polish them frequently.

Combining colours

It takes skill to achieve an attractive combination of light and dark colours, and harmony within the tones. Avoid mixing too many colours unless you have deliberately set out to create a rainbow effect.

You can experiment with a small amount of colourful pattern, but make sure that you dilute it with a lot of plain and uniformly coloured surfaces. Although colours

from opposing sections of the colour spectrum can be brought together to provide an interesting scheme, the choice must be carefully made – because clashing shades may jar and create an unsettling environment.

As a rule, try to choose colours that are within the same family. For example, blue and yellow can be mixed to make green, so those two colours and others closely related to them tend to work well together. Each colour comes in many shades and depths of intensity. Using light

Above, above right and opposite page **Mosaic tiles are a good way to introduce a variety of colours into a bathroom. For example, you can bring warmth to a blue room by adding a few purple tiles. To prevent a scheme becoming too dark, sprinkle** **in a few lighter shades of the main colour, or choose a dark colour for the lower part of the room and fade in lighter and brighter shades of the same colour as the tiles reach the ceiling.**
Left **Accessories also can add touches of vivid colour.**

Right **Blue is a perennially popular colour in bathrooms and shower rooms because of its associations with water. Various shades of blue can be used to good effect in both traditional schemes and when combined with modern materials such as the chrome and concrete shown here.**

Below **A simple contrasting band of tiles relieves the monotony of a plain wall, and using one of the colours in the chequerboard floor ties the scheme together.**
Right **Shower curtains can be used to introduce colour and pattern. The curtain shown here has an outer layer of** dark green velvet, with a paler lining, bringing a sense of luxury to an otherwise simple scheme.
Far right **The standard two-colour chequerboard pattern can be made more complex and interesting by adding more colours and laying them randomly.**

and dark tones of the same main colour is another way to broaden the scope of your decorative scheme. For example, if the main wall areas in your bathroom are a taupe or toffee-beige colour, the ceiling could be painted in a paler shade and the woodwork in a richer one. Darker shades can also be used to create false shadows, which can give depth and emphasis to a feature.

Many contemporary bathrooms tend towards neutral and earthy schemes, using pale colours such as grey, beige and off-white. These soft shades complement white ceramic fixtures, and there is no stark contrast or disharmony with wood, stone, cement or glass surfaces.

Using colour to achieve different effects

If your scheme is predominately chrome, glass or steel – hard, shiny surfaces that may have a cool blue or ice green hue – try adding warmer shades, such as greys and blues with undertones of pink, to counteract the potentially cold effect. To cool down hot colours such as red, orange and bright yellow, combine them with matt surfaces such as slate, stone or wood and darker, neutralizing colours such as grey or black.

Colours are often linked with themes – for example, a Mediterranean-style bathroom would have a strong blue and white base, whereas a Provençal flavour would tend towards terracotta and a warm pink or orange wash. A piece of fabric or a mosaic design may also inspire a colour combination that can be reflected in flooring, tiles and paintwork.

If you are unsure about what colours you want, start with a neutral scheme such as white or cream and then add colour to it – maybe a wall of pink or a panel of blue – and see how you feel about the colour when you have

lived with it for a while. It is easier to build up a colour from a pale base than to lighten one that is heavy and dark. Try to achieve a balance of colour intensity between the various parts of the room such as the ceiling, the walls and the floor. If you have surfaces beside the handbasin, bath or shower enclosure, these should be included in the equation. If you put dark or rich colours on the ceiling and the floor, the two will be optically drawn together, which will make the space seem smaller. If you paint one wall in a deep shade and leave the others lighter, the dark

darker and more solid, so that it appears to be anchored. In a pale scheme avoid dramatically contrasting dark surfaces such as black marble, which will seem heavy beside a white ceramic basin and bath in a white room unless other dark elements – a border or accessories – are included. Look for a softer shade of grey or a marble flecked with white that will harmonize with the rest of the scheme.

Introducing colour can be one of the most enjoyable aspects of decorating or redecorating your bathroom, but any scheme should be carefully thought out and tested. Experiment on a small scale by photocopying a plan or enlarging a photograph of the room and tracing over it, then colouring or painting in the various areas; this will help you to visualize how the finished room would look.

wall will dominate and appear closer to the observer – an effective way of making a long, narrow room seem squarer. If you paint the walls and ceiling the same colour and have a floor covering in a similar shade, there will be little distinction between the various elements of the room. To achieve such an integrated scheme, choose a flooring in the same colour as the walls and ceiling but a tone or two deeper; this will make the ground look

display

The style of objects displayed in a bathroom is usually determined by the overall decorative scheme. Framed prints or a shelf of books might be appropriate in an indulgent bathroom, for example, while shells and pebbles could be used to enhance a seaside theme.

Objects placed on the surfaces and sills of a bathroom should be carefully displayed to avoid the appearance of clutter and mess. There is a general rule that odd numbers of items look better in a group than even numbers. If you have an even number of ceramic jars or similar objects, split them up, putting one or three of them a little way from the main group.

There are good reasons for keeping displays and arrangements away from windows. For example, items placed in front of the window impede the passage of light and restrict access to the window, making it difficult to open and close.

Above left and opposite page **If you plan to display a large number of objects, which would be time-consuming to wipe clean on a regular basis, a glass-fronted cabinet like the one included in this bathroom offers an attractive solution.**

Above and right **Bathrooms are personal and usually private spaces where you can indulge in decorative whims that you might not be able to satisfy in the more public rooms in your home. For example, you could decide to display favourite photographs, prints or paintings, or a collection of old pottery, jars or containers, which might also be used for storage.**

Shapes, colours and textures

Displaying objects of various heights and colours can add interest to a room. Place a tall item at the back of a shelf or ledge, preferably slightly off-centre. Mid-height objects can be arranged in front of it and the smallest in the foreground.

Several items in different shades of the same colour can be displayed so that there is a gradual change in depth of tone. For example, you might have towels ranging in colour from dark green to mid apple green. Stacking them in order according to colour shade makes them more visually agreeable.

In an understated, single-coloured bathroom one colourful object will be the focus of attention, so it should be well displayed. In a white bathroom a red towel will stand out, so the towel should be neatly folded or draped rather than screwed up and left hanging off the side of the bath. In a yellow bathroom a single blue glass bottle could be put on a shelf or surface at around eye level so that the eye is comfortably drawn to it.

Contrasting textures – mixing rough with smooth and heavy with light – will also add to a display. For example, on a shelving system or shelf room divider you could place five white towels on one shelf, an opaque glass vase on another and a bowl of sponges on a third. The velvety warm texture of the towels will contrast with the smooth cool exterior of the glass, which in turn will highlight the uneven, knobbly surface of the sponges.

Do not be afraid of empty space. Sometimes a vacant area can be restful; it may also draw the eye to a different part of the room or to a particular display, and in some cases to a view or decoration beyond. 'Less is more', as the saying goes, and this is especially true in a bathroom.

Plants

Plants can help to absorb extra humidity in a bathroom and make the room feel fresh and alive. They introduce a softer element to a room that tends to be full of hard and angular surfaces. Certain varieties with scented flowers not only look attractive but also add their perfume to the warm air.

Choose plants that enjoy a warm humid environment and, if appropriate, restricted access to daylight. Hardy herbs such as sage, rosemary and thyme can thrive in the bathroom atmosphere; they are scented and attractive and can be used in making face packs and hair rinses.

These herbs can be grown in pots and require minimal maintenance. If they begin to look jaded, take them outdoors to recover in daylight for a couple of weeks during the summer.

Orchids that enjoy humidity can add a luxurious and delicate element. Glossy leaved species such as the castor-oil plant will be content in a cooler bathroom, and the sweetheart plant with its decorative heart-shaped leaves is another bathroom-friendly species. Plants that grow well in the absence of direct sunlight include the prayer plant and ferns such as the sword, lace and feather varieties.

Put the plant in a simple, understated cachepot or container so that the plant rather than its pot is the main feature of the display. The colour of the container could be chosen to tone in with the wall or tile colour, which will help to maintain its anonymity.

Dried flowers and plants are an attractive alternative to living species – and they do not need to be cared for. There are many interesting dried seed pods, grasses and thistle heads that bring an outdoor element indoors as

Below and right **Available in shades ranging from gold to brown, large sponges are not only pleasant to use but also make colourful accessories when dry. Objects that have a natural affinity with water – either the sea or fresh water – will be tolerant of the damp environment of the bathroom.**
Bottom **Two sponges and a couple of sunbaked starfish relieve the monotony of a narrow shelf.**

Left **A classical stone urn with an arrangement of hydrangeas softens the expanse of the basin surround and adds a decorative and indulgent element to what might otherwise be a somewhat clincal effect. Plants and fresh flowers do not generally** respond well to the environment of a bathroom, but dried flowers, such as these, can survive – although they may need to be dusted down from time to time, and taken out into the fresh air and sunshine to recuperate if they start to wilt in the damp air.

Glass, china and shells

Where possible, avoid displaying glass or other types of breakable object unless they are safely placed on a high shelf or well out of the way of the accidental flick of a towel or the sleeve or belt of a dressing gown. Glass and china shards can easily cut exposed skin and it is often difficult to sweep up the tiny splinters that remain on the floor surface or in towelling pile after a breakage.

Placing breakable objects on non-slip or ribbed rubber mats can help to give them extra stability. Alternatively, place them towards the back of a deep shelf. Glass-fronted cupboards will also keep them carefully out of harm's way, but ensure that such a cupboard is in keeping with the general feel of the bathroom rather than resembling a display cabinet that has got lost on its way to the sitting room or kitchen. Some people hang decorative pieces of china on the walls of the bathroom. These are

Left A simple shelf with hooks underneath it offers a practical means of storing and displaying bath-related items. It is ideal for a shower room or steam room, where you may want to brush or pumice the skin during bathing.
Right Dried twigs, three plain vases and a glass decanter make a simple but appealing arrangement on the top of a cabinet.

well as a touch of colour and texture. When purchasing a decorative arrangement, ask if the flowers are treated or varnished. Those that are can withstand the atmosphere of the bathroom; others may fade and droop after repeated exposure to moisture.

When buying coloured dried flowers, be careful to check that the dyes are fast because condensation may cause the colours to leach out and drip onto surfaces and fabrics in the room. Also, if you brush up against the flower arrangement when undressed, you may inadvertently and temporarily dye your skin.

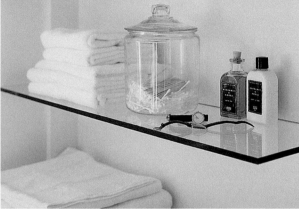

often chosen to reflect the colour or theme of the
bathroom. For example, if pale blue and white Delft-style
tiles have been used for the shower and bath surround,
then plates, or a number of original, antique tiles echoing
the colour and pictorial finish, may be hung and displayed
or stacked on shelves. Similarly, plates with the Willow
Pattern theme can be used in a white and dark blue
bathroom. Wall-hung china is often safer than freestanding items because it is hooked or wired to a fixed
hook or support. These sorts of displays can be quickly
and effectively washed and replaced.

Some people like to exaggerate the watery theme of
a bathroom with displays of shells. These can gather dust
and, being fragile, are often easily broken.

To display shells attractively but safely, you could
consider framing them. Depending of the depth of your
biggest shell, you may need a box frame that has added
capacity. The shells can then be arranged and stuck
onto a painted or coloured background, or even a
background of sand, and then carefully clipped into
the back of the frame.

Sensual pleasures

There are many opportunities in a bathroom to combine visual and aural pleasures. Sensual perfumes such as patchouli, rose and ylang-ylang can be shown on display but also used. Some essences and perfumes may be stored in attractive clear glass bottles and used directly in the bath water or in a massage oil but others that are sensitive to light will have to be kept in a dark place or in coloured glass bottles.

Other ways of using scent to aid relaxation, relieve stress and help insomnia include burning a joss stick or cones of jasmine or sandalwood. These are best used in a stand or dish that is heat-resistant and will catch the cinders and ash as the stick or cone burns. Scented candles have a similar effect and can be bought in containers that have been specially treated to make them resistant to heat.

Candlelight is a very restful and subtle form of illumination in a bathroom, and the candles themselves can be arranged to form an attractive display. Small tea lights placed in the base of coloured glass containers will cause the glass to emit a colourful glow. Tea lights are also relatively safe because the flame and hot wax are kept safely within the container.

Wall sconces are another way of bringing candlelight into the bathroom. These can be displayed on either side of the bath or in rows one above the other. Wall sconces with mirrored backs double the effectiveness of the candle flame.

In a dressing room or en suite bathroom you could make a colourful display of silk ties or silk scarves. Hanging silk in a warm moist environment can help to keep it crease-free, as the humidity and temperature will cause the lines and folds to drop out. But remember that, after someone has indulged in a steamy bath, the room should be ventilated to prevent the silk becoming damp and musty.

One great advantage of displaying small items and objects is that they are not fixed for life. You can always rearrange or vary them to transform a room or give it a fresh look. You may also find that you like to change displays from season to season so that you are in touch with what is going on outdoors. This can be done not simply with the practical trappings such as towels and shower curtains but also with plants and baskets of pine cones or seashells.

Right **A decorative bowl is displayed on a cabinet with scroll detailing: the bowl is a basin and the cabinet conceals pipes and unsightly bits of plumbing.**
Below **Guest soaps can be laid out in a small basket lined with a hand towel.**
Far right **The display of a single stem of a fresh flower in an ornate container with simple pots and bowls on a bamboo tray is an idea inspired by the Orient.**

sources

The manufacturers, designers and retailers who appear in this source directory are included and categorized at the discretion of the author – it is not possible to list every manufacturer and bathroom specialist. Some are mentioned more than once because they make or supply more than one type of product; others are placed in one particular category even though they may also stock or make items in others.

Numbers given are usually for a head office; local agents and stockists may also be available.

BATHROOM COMPANIES

The Bathroom Store
75 Upper Richmond Road
London SW15
020 8870 8888
Also in Fulham and Barnet
Classic and rolltop baths

Bathroom Discount Centre
297 Munster Road
London SW6 6BW
020 7381 4222

Bodywash
433 High Road
Ilford, Essex IGI 1TR
020 8478 1617

Colourwash
165 Chamberlayne Road,
London NW10 3NU
020 8459 8918
Also in London SW6 and
Sunningdale (Berks)
*Wide range of fixtures,
accessories and furniture*

Jacob Delafon
Unit 1, Churchward
Southmead Park
Didcot, Oxon OX11 7HB
01235 510511

Frederick H & Co
143-145 Kew Road
Richmond upon Thames
Surrey TW9 2PN
020 8332 6874

Ideal Standard and Sottini
The Bathroom Works
National Avenue
Kingston upon Hull HU5 4HS
01482 499380

Miscellanea
Crossways, Churt
Farnham, Surrey GU10 2JE
01428 714014
Also in Bournemouth, Risca
(Gwent) and Tring (Herts)
Medieval French to hi-tech

Max Pike
4 Eccleston Street
London SW1W 9LN
020 7730 7206

Original Bathrooms
143-145 Kew Road
Richmond upon Thames
Surrey TW9 2PN
020 8940 7554

Pipe Dreams
70 Gloucester Road
London SW7 4XX
020 7225 3978

Shires Bathrooms
Beckside Road, Bradford
West Yorks BD7 2JE
01274 521199

Submarine,
3 Royal Exchange Court
Glasgow G1 3DB
0141 243 2424

Svedberg of Sweden
717 Fulham Road
London SW6 5UL
020 7371 9215
*Thirty showroom displays;
design service*

**Vernon Tutbury and
B.C. Sanitan**
Silverdale Road, Silverdale
Newcastle under Lyme
Stoke on Trent ST5 6EL
01782 717175

Villeroy & Boch
267 Merton Road
London SW18 5JS
020 8871 4028

Vola (UK)
Unit 12
Ampthill Business Park
Station Road, Ampthill
Beds MK45 2QW
01525 841155

The Water Monopoly
16-18 Lonsdale Road
London NW6 6RD
020 7624 2631

FLOORING

Amtico
Head Office
Kingfield Road
Coventry CV6 5PL
024 7686 1500
*Vinyl flooring; design and
cutting service*

Attica
543 Battersea Park Road
London SW11 3BL
020 7546 2023
*Marble, granite, slate and
terracotta*

Bath and Portland Stone
Moor Parkhouse
Moor Green
Corsham, Wilts SN13 9SE
01255 811234
*Bath and Portland stone in
various sizes and thicknesses*

Country Hardwood
Creech Mill, Mill Lane
Creech St Michael
Taunton, Somerset
TA3 5PX
01823 443760
*White oak and wooden
floors*

First Flooring
174 Wandsworth
Bridge Road
London SW6 2UQ
020 7736 1123
*Industrial and heavy-duty
floor coverings as well
as linoleum*

Forbo-Nairn
PO Box 1, Kirkcaldy
Fife KY1 2SB
01592 643777
*Wide range of linoleum
and vinyl*

Fired Earth
Oxford Road
Adderbury
Oxon OX17 3HP
01295 812088
Other offices around England
and in Dublin, Copenhagen,
Oslo and Gothenburg
*Terracotta and encaustic
tiles, many suitable for
period, traditional and
classic styles*

**The Hardwood
Flooring Co**
146-152 West End Lane
London NW6 1SD
020 7328 8481
*For supply and installation of
Junckers, Kahrs and Tarkett;
also new and reclaimed strip,
blocks, planks, maple, ash,
oak, pine, elm and beech*

Junckers
Wheaton Court
Commercial Centre
Wheaton Road
Witham, Essex CM8 3UJ
01376 517512
Classic wooden floors

LASSCo
(London Architectural
Salvage and Supply Co Ltd)
St Michael's, Mark Street
London EC2A 4ER
020 7739 0448
*New and old reclaimed
wood, Victorian pine boards,
flagstones and terracotta*

Marley Floors
Lenham
Maidstone ME17 2DE
01622 85400
Vinyl flooring

Moutarde
10 Stoney Street
London SE1 9AD
020 7403 4319
Concrete finishes

Paris Ceramics
583 Kings Road
London SW6 2EH
020 7371 7778
*Also in Harrogate, New
York and Los Angeles
English and French
limestone, new and
reclaimed 18th-century
terracotta, mosaic and
ceramic tiles*

Siesta Cork Tile Co
Unit 21, Tait Road
Gloucester Road
Croydon, Surrey CR0 2DP
020 8683 4055
*Wide range of thicknesses
and types of cork*

Sinclair Till
791-793 Wandsworth Road
London SW8 3JQ
020 7720 0031
*Comprehensive selection of
linoleum in a variety of
patterns; custom-design
service, wooden floors, and
natural fibre coverings*

Stone Age
19 Filmer Road
London SW6 7BU
020 7385 7954
*Over 30 types of sandstone
and limestone*

Stonell
521-523 Battersea Park Road
London SW11 3BN
020 7738 0606
Flagstone and stone tiles

Terra Firma Tiles
70 Chalk Farm Road
London NW1 8AN
020 7485 7227
*Good selection of durable
floor tiles*

Walcot Reclamation
108 Walcot Street
Bath BA1 5BG
01225 335532
*Reclaimed wood, flagstone
and quarry tiles*

**CERAMIC TILES AND
SPLASHBACKS**
Ceramica Blue
10 Blenheim Crescent
London W11 1NN
020 7727 0288
*Unusual and brightly
coloured tiles*

Kenneth Clark Ceramics
Southover Grange
Southover Road
Lewes, East Sussex BN7 1TP
01273 476761
*Ranges of individual and
unusual ceramic designs*

Domus Tiles
33 Parkgate Road
London SW11 4NP
020 7223 5555
Ceramic and marble tiles

Formica
Coast Road
North Shields
Tyne & Wear NE29 8RE
0191 259 300
*Easy to wipe and care for, a
classic material back in fashion*

The Life Enhancing Tile Co
Unit 4a, Alliance House
14-28 St Mary's Road
Portsmouth, Hants PO1 5PH
023 9286 2709
*Encaustic tiles, plain and
with unusual design*

Marlborough Tiles
Elcot Lane, Marlborough
Wilts SN8 2AY
01672 512422
Plain and traditional ranges

Merchants
Unit C, Olmar Wharf
Malt Street, London SE1 5AY
020 7237 0060
Suppliers of stainless steel

The Original Tile Company
23a Howe Street
Edinburgh EH3 6TF
0131 556 2013
*Wide variety of tiles
including Victorian-style
and marble*

The Reject Tile Shop
178 Wandsworth
   Bridge Road
London SW6 2UQ
020 7731 6098
*Bargain supplier of ends of
lines, plain and patterned
tiles as well as infill and
borders*

Worlds End Tiles
Railway Gardens Yard
Silverthorne Road
London SW8
020 7720 8358
*Wide range of ceramic
tiles, matt and shiny glaze;
custom-design service*

Stovax
Falcon Road
Sowton Industrial Estate
Exeter, Devon EX2 7LF
01392 474011
Floor and wall tiles

OTHER SURFACES
Bordercraft
Old Forge, Peterchurch
Herefordshire HR2 0SD
01981 550251
*Bespoke hardwood
surfaces*

CD (UK)
Unit 8, Centre 27
Bankwood Way
Birstall, Batley
West Yorks WF17 9TB
01924 424476
*Supplier and distributor
of Corian*

Duropal
131 Peter's Court
Chalfont St Peter
Bucks SL9 9QJ
01753 886557
Laminate supplier

Granite & Marble World
Clarendon House
62-63 Downing Street
Farnham, Surrey GU9 7PN
01252 717979
*Surrounds, tiles and flooring
in granite and marble*

**The Granite Worktop
Company**
PO Box 195, Bolton BL7 0FB
01204 852247
Granite specialist

Hannings Furniture Co
Unit 5/1, The Mews
Brook Street, Mitcheldean
Gloucester GL17 0SL
01594 544196
*Stockists of contemporary
and man-made surfaces*

Kayode Lipede
6 Iroko House
Lithos Road
London NW3 6ER
020 7794 7535
Concrete surfaces

South London Hardwood
Belgrave Road
London SE25 5AW
020 8771 6764
*Oak, ash, mahogany, teak,
pine, maple, elm and pine*

Tops Laminates
Unit 1, Little Tennis Street
South Colwick
Nottingham NG2 4EU
0115 941 9707
*Synthetic products such as
Corian, Cygnautre, Antium,
Marlam and Swanstone*

UK Marble
21 Burcott Road
Hereford HR4 9LW
01432 352178
*Wide range of granite and
marble surfaces*

Whitehall Worksurfaces
Exhibition House
Grape Street
Leeds LS10 1BX
0113 244 4892
*New man-made surfaces,
including Erbistone quartz-
based material and Pyrolave,
made from lava*

SINKS AND TAPS

Armitage Shanks
Armitage, Rugeley
Staffs WS15 4BT
01543 490253
Comprehensive selection

Aston Matthews
141-147 Essex Road
London N1 2SN
020 7226 7220
Good range of traditional and antique items

CP Hart
Newnham Terrace
Hercules Road
London SE1 7DR
020 7902 1000
Wide range; exclusive stockist of Philippe Starck bathrooms Edition 2; also stocks Duravit, Hansgrohe and Hoesch

Vola
Unit 12
Ampthill Business Park
Station Road, Ampthill
Beds MK45 2QW
01525 841155
Sleek modern designs

Pegler
St Catherine's Avenue
Doncaster
South Yorks DN4 8DF
01302 368581.
Tap specialist

BATHS, WHIRLPOOL AND SPA BATHS

Armitage Shanks
Armitage, Rugeley
Staffs WS15 4BT
01543 490253

Hydraspa
Unit 2, Crossgate Drive
Queen's Drive Industrial
Estate, Nottingham
NG2 1LW
01602 866444

Jacuzzi (UK)
17 Mount Street
London W1Y 5RA
020 7409 1776

Ucosan
Roland Moss & Associates
Melville, Bowden House Lane
Wilmslow, Cheshire SK9 2BU
01625 525202
Luxury baths, furniture in Quaryl

SHOWERS

Aquadart
7 Wycliffe Industrial Park
Leicester Road
Lutterworth
Leics LE17 4HG
01455 556561

Aqualisa Products
The Flyers Way
Westerham
Kent TN16 1DE
01959 563240

Caradon Mira
Cromwell Road
Cheltenham
Glos GL52 5EP
01242 221221

Hansgrohe
Unit D2,
Sandown Park Trading Estate
Royal Mills, Esher
Surrey KT10 8BL
01372 465665

Matki
Churchward Road
Yate, Bristol BS37 5PL
01454 322888
Wide range of shower enclosures with lightweight and watertight frames

Nordic
Unit 5, Fairview Estate
Holland Road
Hurst Green, Oxted
Surrey RH8 9BZ
01882 716111

Showeristic
Unit 10
Manor Industrial Estate
Flint, Clwyd CH6 5UY
01352 735381
Made-to-measure shower enclosures to suit non-standard sizes and sloping ceilings

Teuco
Suite 314
Business Design Centre
52 Upper Street
London N1 0QH
020 7704 2190
Hydro showers, whirlpool baths and multifunction showers

Trevi
PO Box 60
National Avenue
Kingston upon Hull
North Humberside HU5 4JE
01482 470788

Triton
Triton House
Newdagate Street
Nuneaton
Warwicks CV11 4EU
01203 344441

Tylo
Gratton Way
Roundswell Industrial Estate
Barnstaple
Devon EX31 3NL
01271 71676
Saunas, steam rooms, steam/shower combinations and spas from Norway

RADIATORS AND TOWEL RAILS

Bisque
244 Belsize Road,
London NW6 4BT
020 7328 2225

Heating World
Excelsior Works, Eyre Street
Birmingham B18 7AD
0121 454 2244
Hot water and electric towel rails

Imperial
Orbital 5, Orbital Way
Cannock, Staffs WS11 3XW
01543 574724

Potterton Myson
Eastern Avenue
Team Valley Trading Estate
Gateshead
Tyne & Wear NE11 0PG
0345 697509
High-efficiency Kickspace convector heater, which fits into small and 'dead' spaces under fitted units or in the floor

Radiating Style
Unit 15
Derby Road Industrial Estate
Hounslow TW30 3NQ
020 8577 9111

Vogue
Units 9 & 10
Strawberry Lane Industrial
Estate, Willenhall
West Midlands WV13 3RS
01902 637330

Walney Warmth
Stanton Square
London SE26 5AB
020 8659 3430
Cast-iron, aluminium and tubular steel radiators

LIGHTING

Atrium
Centrepoint
22-24 St Giles High Street
London WC2H 8LN
020 7379 7288

British Home Stores
129-137 Marylebone Road
London NW1 5QD
Branches in most big towns
Interesting and unusual light fittings at budget prices

Chelsea Lighting Design
1 Woodfall Court
London SW3 4EJ
020 7824 8144
Advice on light installation

John Cullen Lighting
216 Fulham Palace Road
London W6 9NT
020 7371 5400
Professional service and wide range of light fittings

Guzzini
Unit 3
Mitcham Industrial Estate
85 Streatham Road
Mitcham, Surrey CR4 2AP
020 8646 4141
Stylish contemporary designs

London Lighting Company
135 Fulham Road,
London SW3 6RT
020 7589 3612
*A wide range of modern
and work lights*

Mr Light
275 Fulham Road
London SW10 9PZ
020 7352 7525
*Contemporary and
traditional fittings*

Christopher Wray
591-593 Kings Road,
London SW6 2YW
020 7736 8434
Branches in many major UK
towns and in Hyogo, Japan
*Wide range from modern
to traditional*

FURNITURE
Hayloft
3 Bond Street
London W4 1QZ
020 8747 3510
*Custom-made furniture in
hardwoods, old pine, MDF*

Ikea
255 North Circular Road
London NW13 0JQ
020 8208 5600 for branches
and catalogue details
*In-store computer-generated
images indicate how your
bathroom will look; self-
assembly units or delivery
and installation available*

John Lewis of Hungerford
Park Street, Hungerford
Berks RG17 OEF
01488 682066
*Well-established company
with a good range of
designs*

Martin Moore & Co
28 Church Street, Altrincham
Cheshire WA14 4DW
0161 928 2643
*Designs in hardwoods and
reclaimed timbers*

Turner & Foye
87 High Street, Esher
Surrey KT10 9QA
01372 470800
*Furniture made to
commission*

ACCESSORIES
Aero
96 Westbourne Grove
London W2 5RT
020 7221 1950
Own-design bath accessories

The Bath House,
Liberty
210-20 Regent Street
London W1R 6AH
020 7734 1234
*Towels, bath mats, shower
curtains and accessories*

Black Country Heritage
Britannia House, Mill Street
Brierley Hill
West Midlands DY5 2TH
01384 480810
*Bathracks, toothbrush
holders and other metal-
based accessories*

Cologne & Cotton
791 Fulham Road,
London SW6 5HD
020 7736 9261
Also in Leamington Spa
*Towels, linen guest towels
and robes*

Czech & Speake
39c Jermyn Street
London SW1Y 6DN
020 8980 4567
*Toiletries and traditional-
style bathroom fittings*

Descamps
197 Sloane Street
London SW1X 9QX
020 7235 6957
*Wide range of bathrobes
and towels in many colours
and styles*

The Holding Company
243-245 King's Road London
SW3 5EL
020 7352 1600
*Cupboards and storage
for small bathrooms*

The Linen Merchant
11 Montpelier Street
London SW7 1EX
020 7584 3654

Muji
26 Great Marlborough Street
London W1V 1HL
020 7494 1197
*Airtight opaque plastic
storage containers and
oriental kitchen accessories*

Inventory
26-40 Kensington
  High Street
London W8 4PF
020 7937 2626
*Well-priced ranges of kitchen
gadgets, china and storage*

River Accessories
0990 696969
*Comprehensive
mail-order catalogue*

Stiffkey Bathrooms
Stiffkey, Wells-next-the-Sea
Norfolk NR23 1AJ
01328 830084

Samuel Heath
Cobden Works
Leopold Street
Birmingham B12 0UJ
0121 772 2303

Lance Roberts
Period Mirrors
Unit 12, Hockley Industrial
Centre, Hooley Lane
Redhill, Surrey RH1 6JF
01737 767430

The Looking Glass of Bath
96 Walcot Street
Bath BA1 5BG
01225 461969
*Specialist mirror shop; styles
can be made to order*

Overmantles of Battersea
66 Battersea Bridge Road,
London SW11 3G
020 7223 8151
*Large selection of traditional-
style mirrors*

UFO
291 Deansgate
Manchester M3 4EW
0161 839 1699
Contemporary mirrors

BATH RE-ENAMELLING
**Bath Re-enamelling
Service**
Chapel Court
70 Hospital Street
Nantwich
Cheshire CW5 5RF
01270 626554

The Bath Doctor
Prospect House
Canterbury Road, Challock
Ashford, Kent TN25 4BB
01233 740532

Renubath Services
248 Lillie Road
London SW6 7QA
020 7381 8337

ORGANIZATIONS
British Bathroom Council
Federation House
Station Road
Stoke on Trent ST4 2RT
01782 747074

British Ceramic Research
Queens Road, Penkhull
Stoke on Trent ST4 7LQ
01782 45431

**British Ceramic Tile
Council**
Federation House
Station Road
Stoke on Trent ST4 2RT
01782 747147
*Association of UK ceramic
and quarry tile manufactures*

**Disability Information
Trust**
Mary Marlborough Centre
Nuffield Orthopaedic Centre
Headington
Oxford OX3 7LD
01865 227592

**Disabled Living
Foundation**
380-384 Harrow Road
London W9 2HU
020 7289 6111

Institute of Plumbing
64 Station Lane
Hornchurch RM12 6NB
01708 472791

acknowledgements

Key: **t** = top, **b** = below, **l** = left, **r** = right, **c** = centre

Endpapers Gabriele Sanders' apartment in New York; **1** Karen Davies' apartment in London designed by Joëlle Darby; **2** an apartment in Paris designed by Bruno Tanquerel; **4** a house in Surrey refurbished by Damien D'Arcy Associates; **7** a house in Surrey refurbished by Damien D'Arcy Associates; **8** a house in Hampstead, London designed by Orefelt Associates; **9** Gabriele Sanders' apartment in New York; **10–11** a house in Paris designed by Bruno Tanquerel; **11** a house in London designed by Carden & Cunietti; **12** a house in Surrey refurbished by Damien D'Arcy Associates; **13 l** Alison Thompson & Billy Paulett's house in London designed by Stephen Turvil Architects; **13 cl** & **cr** a house in Highbury, London designed by Dale Loth Architects; **13 r** Stephan Schulte's loft apartment in London; **14–15** House in London by Seth Stein; **16 l** a house in Surrey refurbished by Damien D'Arcy Associates; **16 r** & **17** a house in Hampstead, London designed by Orefelt Associates; **18 t** Simon Crookall's apartment in London designed by Urban Salon Ltd; **18 b** 'Manhattan Loft' designed by Bruce Bierman Design, Inc.; **19 t** Interior Designer Alan Tanksley's own apartment in Manhattan; **19 bl** & **br** Alison Thompson & Billy Paulett's house in London designed by Stephen Turvil Architects; **20 t** Philippa Rose's house in London designed by Caroline Paterson/Victoria Fairfax of Paterson Gornall Interiors, together with Clive Butcher Designs; **20 b** a house in Paris designed by Bruno Tanquerel; **21** Emma & Neil's house in London, walls painted by Garth Carter; **22** Hilton McConnico's house near Paris; **23** Kenneth Hirst's apartment in New York; **24** House in London by Seth Stein; **25** Richard Oyarzarbal's apartment in London designed by Jeff Kirby of Urban Research Laboratory; **26** Calvin Tsao & Zack McKown's apartment in New York designed by Tsao & McKown; **27** House in London by Seth Stein; **28** a house in London designed by Carden & Cunietti; **29** Calvin Tsao & Zack McKown's apartment in New York designed by Tsao & McKown; **30–31** John Eldridge's loft apartment in London designed by Seth Stein; **32 t** Andrew Wilson's house in London designed by Azman Owens; **32 b** & **33–34** a house in Surrey refurbished by Damien D'Arcy Associates; **35** the Sugarman–Behun house on Long Island; **36–37** a house in Surrey refurbished by Damien D'Arcy Associates; **37 t** Suzanne Slesin & Michael Steinberg's apartment in New York – design by Jean-Louis Ménard; **38** Sera Hersham-Loftus' house in London; **39 l** architect's house in London designed by Dale Loth Architects; **39 cr** a house in Hampstead, London designed by Orefelt Associates; **39 r** an apartment in Paris designed by Bruno Tanquerel; **40 l** & **40–41** Philippa Rose's house in London designed by Caroline Paterson/Victoria Fairfax of Paterson Gornall Interiors, together with Clive Butcher Designs; **41 l** an apartment in New York designed by Nasser Nakib Architect & Bunny Williams Inc. Decorator; **41 r** Sera Hersham-Loftus' house in London; **43** a house in Paris designed by Bruno Tanquerel; **44–45** Lulu Guinness' house in London; **46** Freddie Daniells' apartment in London designed by Brookes Stacey Randall; **47 tl** Interior Designer Alan Tanksley's own apartment in Manhattan; **47 tr** an apartment in New York designed by David Deutsch & Sidnam Petrone Gartner Architects; **47 br** John Minshaw's house in London designed by John Minshaw; **48 t** Sera Hersham-Loftus' house in London; **48 cl** & **cr** & **48–49** Emma & Neil's house in London, walls painted by Garth Carter; **50** & **51 l** Sera Hersham-Loftus' house in London; **51 r** John Minshaw's house in London designed by John Minshaw; **52** Tim Attias' apartment in London designed by Stickland Coombe Architecture; **53 t** an apartment in Paris designed by Bruno Tanquerel; **53 b** & **54** a house in Hampstead, London designed by Orefelt Associates; **55** House in London by Seth Stein; **56 l** Richard Hopkin's apartment in London designed by HM2; **56 r** & **57** Freddie Daniells' apartment in London designed by Brookes Stacey Randall; **58–59** Calvin Tsao & Zack McKown's apartment in New York designed by Tsao & McKown; **60 l** a house in Surrey refurbished by Damien D'Arcy Associates; **60 r** the Sugarman–Behun house on Long Island; **61 tl** Freddie Daniells' apartment in London designed by Brookes Stacey Randall; **61 bl** & **r** a house in Surrey refurbished by Damien D'Arcy Associates; **62** Richard Hopkin's apartment in London designed by HM2; **63** a house in Surrey refurbished by Damien D'Arcy Associates; **64** a house in London designed by John Minshaw; **65 tl** & **tr** a house in Surrey refurbished by Damien D'Arcy Associates; **65 br** John Eldridge's loft apartment in London designed by Seth Stein; **66** & **67** House in London by Seth Stein; **68** Simon Brignall & Christina Rosetti's loft apartment in London designed by David Mikhail Architects; **69** John Eldridge's loft apartment in London designed by Seth Stein; **70** & **71 tl** Fred Wadsworth's flat in London designed by Littman Goddard Hogarth; **71 bl** an apartment in Paris designed by Bruno Tanquerel; **71 br** Andrew Wilson's house in London designed by Azman Owens; **72** One New Inn Square, a private dining room and home of chef David Vanderhook, all enquiries 020 7729 3645; **73** Jacques & Laurence Hintzy's apartment near Paris designed by Paul Mathieu; **74–75** New York City apartment designed by Marino + Giolito; **76–77** Karen Davies' apartment in London designed by Joëlle Darby; **78 l** Sera Hersham-Loftus' house in London; **78 r** architect's house in London designed by Dale Loth Architects; **79** Gomez/Murphy Loft, Hoxton, London designed by Urban Salon Ltd; **80** Calvin Tsao & Zack McKown's apartment in New York designed by Tsao & McKown; **81 tl** an apartment in Paris designed by Bruno Tanquerel; **81 bl** Karen Davies' apartment in London designed by Joëlle Darby; **81 r** an apartment in New York designed by David Deutsch & Sidnam Petrone Gartner Architects; **82** a house in Holland Park, London; **83** Mr & Mrs Jeremy Lascelles' house in London designed by Carden & Cunietti; **84 l** & **tr** Richard Hopkin's apartment in London designed by HM2; **85** One New Inn Square, a private dining room and home of chef David Vanderhook, all enquiries 020 7729 3645; **86** the Sugarman–Behun house on Long Island; **87** Stephan Schulte's loft apartment in London; **88–89** Architect Nigel Smith's apartment in London; **90 t** Gomez/Murphy Loft, Hoxton, London designed by Urban Salon Ltd; **90 b** architect's house in London designed by Dale Loth Architects; **91** Stephan Schulte's loft apartment in London; **92–93** Calvin Tsao & Zack McKown's apartment in New York designed by Tsao & McKown; **93** Karen Davies' apartment in London designed by Joëlle Darby; **94** Suzanne Slesin & Michael Steinberg's apartment in New York – design by Jean-Louis Ménard; **95 cl** a house in Highbury, London designed by Dale Loth Architects; **95 r** Jacques & Laurence Hintzy's apartment near Paris designed by Paul Mathieu; **96–97** Heidi Wish & Philip Wish's apartment in London designed by Moutarde & Heidi Wish; **97 cl** a house in Paris designed by Bruno Tanquerel; **97 bl** Tiffany Ogden's house in London designed by Andy Martin of

Fin Architects & Designers; **97 r** architect's house in London designed by Dale Loth Architects; **98** Alison Thompson & Billy Paulett's house in London designed by Stephen Turvil Architects; **99** 'Manhattan Loft' designed by Bruce Bierman Design, Inc.; **100** a house in Surrey refurbished by Damien D'Arcy Associates; **101 tl** John Minshaw's house in London designed by John Minshaw; **101 tr, bl** & **br** a house in Surrey refurbished by Damien D'Arcy Associates; **102 l** Andrew Wilson's house in London designed by Azman Owens; **102 tr** & **103** Simon Brignall & Christina Rosetti's loft apartment in London designed by David Mikhail Architects; **102 br** Richard Hopkin's apartment in London designed by HM2; **104–105** Philippa Rose's house in London designed by Caroline Paterson/Victoria Fairfax of Paterson Gornall Interiors, together with Clive Butcher Designs; **105 tl** Vicente Wolf's home on Long Island; **105 tr** Paul Brazier & Diane Lever's house in London designed by Carden & Cunietti; **105 br** Mark Kirkley & Harumi Kaijima's house in Sussex; **106** Calvin Tsao & Zack McKown's apartment in New York designed by Tsao & McKown; **107 tl** Freddie Daniells' apartment in London designed by Brookes Stacey Randall; **107 tc** & **tr** Richard Hopkin's apartment in London designed by HM2; **107 b** a house in Surrey refurbished by Damien D'Arcy Associates; **108 l** Emma & Neil's house in London, walls painted by Garth Carter; **108 r** Calvin Tsao & Zack McKown's apartment in New York designed by Tsao & McKown; **108–109** Heidi Wish & Philip Wish's apartment in London designed by Moutarde & Heidi Wish; **109 r** a house in Paris designed by Bruno Tanquerel; **110 tl** a house in Paris designed by Bruno Tanquerel; **110 bl** One New Inn Square, a private dining room and home of chef David Vanderhook, all enquiries 020 7729 3645; **110–111** Simon Brignall & Christina Rosetti's loft apartment in London designed by David Mikhail Architects; **111 t** Simon Crookall's apartment in London designed by Urban Salon Ltd; **111 b** Architect Nigel Smith's apartment in London; **112 tl** & **br** a house in Surrey refurbished by Damien D'Arcy Associates; **112 tr** Jacques & Laurence Hintzy's apartment near Paris designed by Paul Mathieu; **112 bc** Sara Horsham Loftus' house in London; **113 t** Richard Hopkin's apartment in London designed by HM2; **113 bl** a house in Highbury, London designed by Dale Loth Architects; **113 br** Emma & Neil's house in London, walls painted by Garth Carter; **114 l** Karen Davies' apartment in London designed by Joëlle Darby; **114 c** Gabriele Sanders' apartment in New York; **114 r** a house in Paris designed by Bruno Tanquerel; **115** Jacques & Laurence Hintzy's apartment near Paris designed by Paul Mathieu; **116 l** Andrew Wilson's house in London designed by Azman Owens; **116 r** & **117 l** Stephan Schulte's loft apartment in London; **117 r** Gabriele Sanders' apartment in New York; **118** John Eldridge's loft apartment in London designed by Seth Stein; **119 tl** New York City apartment designed by Marino + Giolito; **119 tc** One New Inn Square, a private dining room and home of chef David Vanderhook, all enquiries 020 7729 3645; **119 tr** an apartment in New York designed by David Deutsch & Sidnam Petrone Gartner Architects; **119 cl** Philippa Rose's house in London designed by Caroline Paterson/Victoria Fairfax of Paterson Gornall Interiors, together with Clive Butcher Designs; **119 c** Heidi Wish & Philip Wish's apartment in London designed by Moutarde & Heidi Wish; **119 cr** Alison Thompson & Billy Paulett's house in London designed by Stephen Turvil Architects; **119 bl** & **bc** a house in Paris designed by Bruno Tanquerel; **119 br** Suzanne Slesin & Michael Steinberg's apartment in New York – design by Jean-Louis Ménard; **120 l** Paul Brazier & Diane Lever's house in London designed by Carden & Cunietti;

120 tr One New Inn Square, a private dining room and home of chef David Vanderhook, all enquiries 020 7729 3645; **120 cr** an apartment in New York designed by Nasser Nakib Architect & Bunny Williams Inc. Decorator; **120 br** Richard Oyarzarbal's apartment in London designed by Jeff Kirby of Urban Research Laboratory; **121 t** Architect Nigel Smith's apartment in London; **121 b** Richard Oyarzarbal's apartment in London designed by Jeff Kirby of Urban Research Laboratory; **122** & **123 l** a house in Hampstead, London designed by Orefelt Associates; **123 r** Freddie Daniells' apartment in London designed by Brookes Stacey Randall; **124 tl** Interior Designer Alan Tanksley's own apartment in Manhattan; **124 tr** Kenneth Hirst's apartment in New York; **124 b** Mark Kirkley & Harumi Kaijima's house in Sussex; **125 t** & **bl** a house in Holland Park, London; **125 br** 'Manhattan Loft' designed by Bruce Bierman Design, Inc.; **126** a house in Surrey refurbished by Damien D'Arcy Associates; **127 t** Paul Brazier & Diane Lever's house in London designed by Carden & Cunietti; **127 c** One New Inn Square, a private dining room and home of chef David Vanderhook, all enquiries 020 7729 3645; **127 b** New York City apartment designed by Marino + Giolito; **128** House in London by Seth Stein; **128–129** a house in Surrey refurbished by Damien D'Arcy Associates; **129 t** a house in Paris designed by Bruno Tanquerel; **129 b** 'Manhattan Loft' designed by Bruce Bierman Design, Inc.; **130** a house in Surrey refurbished by Damien D'Arcy Associates; **131 l** Kenneth Hirst's apartment in New York; **131 r** a house in London designed by Carden & Cunietti; **132 t** Vicente Wolf's home on Long Island; **132 b** Lulu Guinness' house in London; **133 t** a house in Paris designed by Bruno Tanquerel; **133 r** Paul Brazier & Diane Lever's house in London designed by Carden & Cunietti; **134 tl** & **tr** a house in Surrey refurbished by Damien D'Arcy Associates; **134 bl** Simon Brignall & Christina Rosetti's loft apartment in London designed by David Mikhail Architects; **134 br** Lulu Guinness' house in London; **135 t** Vicente Wolf's home on Long Island; **135 c** an apartment in New York designed by Nasser Nakib Architect & Bunny Williams Inc. Decorator; **135 b** Alison Thompson & Billy Paulett's house in London designed by Stephen Turvil Architects; **136 tl** & **tr** houses in Paris designed by Bruno Tanquerel; **136 b** Heidi Wish & Philip Wish's apartment in London designed by Moutarde & Heidi Wish; **137** a house in London designed by Carden & Cunietti; **138 tl** Simon Crookall's apartment in London designed by Urban Salon Ltd; **138 tr** New York City apartment designed by Marino + Giolito; **138 bl** Interior Designer Alan Tanksley's own apartment in Manhattan; **138 br** Philippa Rose's house in London designed by Caroline Paterson/Victoria Fairfax of Paterson Gornall Interiors, together with Clive Butcher Designs; **139 tl** a house in Highbury, London designed by Dale Loth Architects; **139 tr** John Minshaw's house in London designed by John Minshaw; **139 bl** Richard Oyarzarbal's apartment in London designed by Jeff Kirby of Urban Research Laboratory; **139 br** Freddie Daniells' apartment in London designed by Brookes Stacey Randall; **140 tl** John Eldridge's loft apartment in London designed by Seth Stein; **140 cl** Jacques & Laurence Hintzy's apartment near Paris designed by Paul Mathieu; **140 tr** Suzanne Slesin & Michael Steinberg's apartment in New York – design by Jean-Louis Ménard; **140 bl** an apartment in New York designed by Nasser Nakib Architect & Bunny Williams Inc. Decorator; **140 bc** Philippa Rose's house in London designed by Caroline Paterson/Victoria Fairfax of Paterson Gornall Interiors, together with Clive Butcher Designs; **140 br** Kenneth Hirst's apartment in New York; **141 t** Suzanne Slesin & Michael

Steinberg's apartment in New York – design by Jean-Louis Ménard; **141 bl** a house in London designed by John Minshaw; **141 br** a house in Paris designed by Bruno Tanquerel; **142–143** Lulu Guinness' house in London; **143** New York City apartment designed by Marino + Giolito; **145 l** a house in Paris designed by Bruno Tanquerel; **145 cl** Hilton McConnico's house near Paris; **145 cr** John Minshaw's house in London designed by John Minshaw; **145 r** 'Manhattan Loft' designed by Bruce Bierman Design, Inc.; **146–147** Gomez/Murphy Loft, Hoxton, London designed by Urban Salon Ltd; **148 t** Stephan Schulte's loft apartment in London; **148 bl** 'Manhattan Loft' designed by Bruce Bierman Design, Inc. **148 br** John Minshaw's house in London designed by John Minshaw; **149 l** a house in Paris designed by Bruno Tanquerel; **149 r** the Sugarman–Behun house on Long Island; **150 t** Richard Hopkin's apartment in London designed by HM2; **150 b** Stephan Schulte's loft apartment in London; **151 tl** Heidi Wish & Philip Wish's apartment in London designed by Moutarde & Heidi Wish; **151 bl** One New Inn Square, a private dining room and home of chef David Vanderhook, all enquiries 020 7729 3645; **151 r** Vicente Wolf's home on Long Island; **152 tl** architect's house in London designed by Dale Loth Architects; **152 tr** & **153** Paul Brazier & Diane Lever's house in London designed by Carden & Cunietti; **152 b** Jacques & Laurence Hintzy's apartment near Paris designed by Paul Mathieu; **154 t** New York City apartment designed by Marino + Giolito; **154 bl** Simon Crookall's apartment in London designed by Urban Salon Ltd.; **154 br** Fred Wadsworth's flat in London designed by Littman Goddard Hogarth; **155** & **156–157** John Minshaw's house in London designed by John Minshaw; **157 b** Frazer Cunningham's house in London; **158 l** Kenneth Hirst's apartment in New York; **158 r** a house in London designed by Carden & Cunietti; **159** Simon Brignall & Christina Rosetti's loft apartment in London designed by David Mikhail Architects; **160 l** Andrew Wilson's apartment in London designed by Azman Owens; **160 r** a house in Surrey refurbished by Damien D'Arcy Associates; **161 bl** a house in

Paris designed by Bruno Tanquerel; **161 t** & **br** Gomez/Murphy Loft, Hoxton, London designed by Urban Salon Ltd; **162 l** Suzanne Slesin & Michael Steinberg's apartment in New York – design by Jean-Louis Ménard; **162 r** a house in London designed by John Minshaw; **163 t** a house in Holland Park, London; **163 bl** New York City apartment designed by Marino + Giolito; **163 br** Vicente Wolf's home on Long Island; **164** an apartment in New York designed by Nasser Nakib Architect & Bunny Williams Inc. Decorator; **165** an apartment in New York designed by David Deutsch & Sidnam Petrone Gartner Architects; **166** Hilton McConnico's house near Paris; **166–167** Heidi Wish & Philip Wish's apartment in London designed by Moutarde & Heidi Wish; **168** & **169** houses in Paris designed by Bruno Tanquerel; **170 tl** & **r** Richard Oyarzarbal's apartment in London designed by Jeff Kirby of Urban Research Laboratory; **171** Paul Brazier & Diane Lever's house in London designed by Carden & Cunietti; **172 t** House in London by Seth Stein; **172 b** Vicente Wolf's home on Long Island; **173 l** a house in London designed by Carden & Cunietti; **174** & **175 tl** Suzanne Slesin & Michael Steinberg's apartment in New York – design by Jean-Louis Ménard; **175 tr** Vicente Wolf's home on Long Island; **175 b** 'Manhattan Loft' designed by Bruce Bierman Design, Inc.; **176–177** the Sugarman–Behun house on Long Island; **178 t** Vicente Wolf's home on Long Island; **178 bl** Calvin Tsao & Zack McKown's apartment in New York designed by Tsao & McKown; **178 br** Hilton McConnico's house near Paris; **179 tl** architect's house in London designed by Dale Loth Architects; **179 tr** John Minshaw's house in London designed by John Minshaw; **179 b** a house in Paris designed by Bruno Tanquerel; **180 t** Frazer Cunningham's house in London; **181** Vicente Wolf's home on Long Island; **192** an apartment in Paris designed by Bruno Tanquerel.

Author's acknowledgments: Many thanks to David Jones of Colourwash and Jenny Hildreth, The Building Design Centre.

Architects and designers whose work is featured in this book:

Alan Tanksley, Inc.
Interior Design
114 East 32nd Street
Suite 1406
New York, New York 10016
USA
t. +1 212 481 8454
f. +1 212 481 8456
19 t, 47 tl, 124 tl, 138 bl

Andy Martin
Fin Architects and Designers
73 Wells Street
London W1P 3RD
e. finbox@globalnet.co.uk
97 bl

Azman Owens
Architects
8 St Albans Place
London N1 0NX
t. 020 7354 2955
f. 020 7354 2966
32 t, 71 br, 102 l, 116 l, 160 l

behun/ziff design
153 E. 53rd Street
43rd Floor
New York, NY 10022
USA   .
t. +1 212 292 6233
f. +1 212 292 6790
Pages 35, 60r, 86, 149r, 176–177

Brookes Stacey Randall
16 Winchester Walk
London SE1 9AQ
t. 020 7403 0707
f. 020 7403 0880
e. info@bsr-architects.com
www.bsr-architects.com
46, 56 r & 57, 61 tl, 107 tl, 123 r, 139 br

Bruce Bierman Design, Inc.
29 West 15 Street
New York, New York 10011
t. +1 212 243 1935
f. +1 212 243 6615
USA
18 b, 99, 125 br, 129 b, 145 r, 148 bl, 175 b

Bruno Tanquerel
Artist
2 Passage St. Sébastien
75011 Paris
France
t. +33 1 43 57 03 93
2, 10–11, 20 b, 39 r, 43, 53 t, 71 bl, 81 tl, 97 cl, 109 r, 110 tl, 114 r, 119 bl &bc, 129 t, 133 t, 136 tl & tr, 141 br, 145 l, 149 l, 161 bl, 168, 169, 179 b, 192

Carden Cunietti
83 Westbourne Park Road
London W2 5QH
t. 020 7229 8559
f. 020 7229 8799
w. www.carden-cunietti.com
11, 28, 83, 105 tr, 120 l, 127 t, 131 r, 133 r, 137, 152 tr, 153, 158 r, 171, 173 l

Caroline Paterson
Paterson Gornall Interiors
50 Lavender Gardens
London SW11 1DN
t. 020 7738 2530
f. 020 7652 0410
20 t, 41, 104–105, 119 cl, 138 br, 140 bc

Clive Butcher Designs
The Granary
The Quay
Wivenhoe
Essex CO7 9BU
t./f. 01206 827708
**20 t, 41, 104–105, 119 cl,
138 br, 140 bc**

Dale Loth Architects
1 Cliff Road
London NW1 9AJ
t. 020 7485 4003
f. 020 7284 4490
e. mail@
dalelotharchitects.ltd.uk
**13 cl & cr, 39 l, 78 r, 90 b,
95 cl, 97 r, 113 bl, 139 tl,
152 tl, 179 tl**

Damien D'Arcy Associates
9 Lamington Street
London W6 0HU
t. 020 8741 1193
f. 020 8563 7784
**4, 12, 16 l, 32 b, 33–34,
36–37, 60 l, 61 bl & r, 63, 65 tl
& tr, 100, 101 tr, bl & br, 107
b, 112 tl & br, 126, 128–129,
130, 134 tl & tr, 160 r**

David Mikhail Architects
Unit 29
1–13 Adler Street
London E1 1EE
t. 020 7377 8424
f. 020 7377 5791
www.davidmikhail.com
**68, 102 tr, 103, 110–111,
134 bl, 159,**

Garth Carter
Specialist interiors painter
t. 0958 412953
21, 48–49, 108 l, 113 br

Heidi Wish and Philip Wish
Interior Design & Build
t./f. 020 7684 8789
**96–97, 108–109, 119 c, 136 b,
151 tl, 166–167**

Hilton McConnico
Interior home designer
8 rue Antoine Panier
93170 Bagnolet
France
t. +33 1 43 62 53 16
f. +33 1 43 62 73 44
e. hmc@club-internet.fr
22, 145 cl, 166, 178 br

Hirst Pacific Ltd.
250 Lafayette Street
New York, New York 10012
USA
t. +1 212 625 3670
f. +1 212 625 3673
e. hirstpacific@earthlink.net
23, 124 tr, 131 l, 140 br, 158 l

HM2
Architects
Richard Webb, Project
Director
Andrew Hanson, Director
33–37 Charterhouse Square
London EC1M 6EA
t. 020 7600 5151
f. 020 7600 1092
e. andrew.hanson@harper-
mackay.co.uk
**56 l, 62, 84 l &tr, 102 br,
107 tc & tr, 113 t, 150 t**

Jean-Louis Ménard
Architect
t/f. + 33 1 46 34 44 92
**37 t, 94, 119 br, 140 tr, 141 t,
162 l, 174, 175 tl**

**Jeff Kirby/Urban Research
Laboratory**
Ground Floor
Lime Wharf
Vyner Street
London E2 9DJ
t. 020 8709 9060
e. info@urbanresearchlab.com
www.urbanresearchlab.com
**25, 120 br, 121 b, 139 bl,
170 tl & r**

Joëlle Darby
Architect
Darby Maclellan Partnership
Unit 3, Limehouse Cut
46 Morris Road
London E14 6NQ
t. 020 7987 4432
e. darby.maclellan@
tinyonline.co.uk
1, 76–77, 81 bl, 93, 114 l

John Minshaw
Architectural Interior
Designer
John Minshaw Designs Ltd
t. 020 7258 0627
f. 020 7258 0628
**47 br, 51 r, 64, 101 tl, 139 tr,
141 bl, 145 cr, 148 br, 155,
156–157, 162 r, 179 tr**

Littman Goddard Hogarth
Architects
12 Chelsea Wharf
15 Lots Road
London SW10 0QJ
t. 020 7351 7871
f. 020 7351 4110
w. www.lgharchitects.co.uk
70, 71 tl, 154 br

Marino + Giolito
161 West 16th Street
New York, NY 10011
USA
t./f. +1 212 675 5737
**74–75, 119 tl, 127 b, 138 tr,
143, 154 t, 163 bl**

Mark Kirkley
Designer and manufacturer
of interior metalwork
t./f. 01424 812613

**Nasser Nakib Architect
& Bunny Williams Inc.**
Decorator
306 East 61st Street
Fifth Floor
New York, New York 10021
USA
t. +1 212 759 1515
f. +1 212 759 1612
41 l, 120 cr, 135 c, 140 bl, 164

Nigel Smith
t. +44 20 7278 8802
e. n-smith@dircon.co.uk
88–89, 111 b, 121 t

Orefelt Associates
Design team: Gunnar Orefelt,
John Massey, Gianni
Botsford, Jason Griffiths
4 Portobello Studios
5 Haydens Place
London W11 1LY
t. 020 7243 3181
f. 020 7792 1126
e. orefelt@msn.com
**8, 16 r, 17, 39 cr, 53 b, 54,
122, 123 l**

Paul Mathieu
Interior Design
France:
12 rue Matheron
13100 Aix-en-Provence
t. +33 4 42 23 97 77
f. +33 4 42 23 97 59
USA:
7 East 14th Street, # 805
New York, New York 10003
t. +1 646 638 4531
**73, 95 r, 112 tr, 115, 140 cl,
152 b**

Sera Hersham-Loftus
'Rude' designer &
lampshade maker
t. 020 7286 5948
**38, 41 r, 48 t, 50, 51 l, 78 l,
112 bc**

Seth Stein
Architect
15 Grand Union Centre
West Row
Ladbroke Grove
London W10 5AS
t./f. 020 8968 8581
e. admin@sethstein.com
w. www.sethstein.com
**14–15, 24, 27, 30–31, 55,
65 br, 66, 67, 69, 118, 128,
140 tl, 172 t**

**Sidnam Petrone Gartner
Architects**
Coty Sidnam, Bill Petrone,
and Eric Gartner
136 West 21st Street
New York, New York 10011
USA
t. +1 212 366 5500
f. +1 212 366 6559
e. sidnampetr@aol.com
47 tr, 81 r, 119 tr, 165

Stephen Turvil Architects
41 Avondale Rise
London SE15 4AJ
t. 020 7639 2212
e. Turv@space1.demon.co.uk
**13 l, 19 bl & br, 98, 119 cr,
135 b**

**Stickland Coombe
Architecture**
258 Lavender Hill
London SW11 1LJ
t. 020 7924 1699
52

Tsao & McKown
Architects
20 Vandam Street
10th Floor
New York, New York 10013
USA
t. +1 212 337 3800
f. +1 212 337 0013
**26, 29, 58–59, 80, 92–93, 106,
108 r, 178 bl**

Urban Salon
Architects
Unit D
Flat Iron Yard
Ayres Street
London SE1 1ES
t. 020 7357 8800
**18 t, 79, 90 t, 111 t, 138 tl,
146–147, 154 bl, 161 t & br**

Vicente Wolf Associates, Inc.
333 West 39th Street
New York, New York 10018
USA
t. +1 212 465 0590
**105 tl, 132 t, 135 t, 151 r, 163
br, 172 b, 175 tr, 178 t, 181**

index

A

Aalto, Alvar: Model 43
  132
accessories 135–41
  in small spaces 75
  wet rooms 89
  see also display
appliances 114–23
  see also taps and spouts
archways 45, 72
Armitage Shanks Sensorflow
  56–8
Armourcast 147
Axor Hansgrohe group 39
  overflow and tap 56

B

bath board 17
bath rack 137
bathmats 64, 141
baths 104–8
  cast-iron 24, 32, 104–5
  ceramic 74
  copper 50–1, 105
  corner 19, 38, 42
  double-ended 42, 107
  freestanding 28, 40–1, 42,
  104–5, 107
  installing antique baths
  31
  Japanese-inspired baths
  39, 105
  planning considerations
  14–17, 21, 24
  restoring/reconditioning
  104–5
  rolltop 41, 42, 105,
  107
  for small spaces 75–7
  steel 56
  streamlined 55–6
  sunken 25, 62
  walk-in 17
  see also spa/whirlpool
  baths; taps and spouts
blinds 63
Breuer, Marcel: chair No 313
  132
bubble bath 53

C

candles/candlelight 61, 100,
  180
carpets 157–8
chaise longue 18, 42, 131
chandeliers 100–2
children and teenagers:
  planning considerations 14,
  16, 78, 113
  furniture 131
cleaning 51, 150–1
  carpet 157–8
  grouting 153, 155
  metals 150
  pipework 53
  planning considerations 24
  wooden floors 162
cloakrooms 68, 78
  planning 17
  siting 23
Cobra-therm radiator 123
colour 38–9, 152, 166–73
  of artificial lighting 96
  black and white 51, 163
  combining 170–1
  cream/brown/black 169–70
  displayed objects 176
  flooring 48
  indulgent bathrooms 45–9,
  51
  pinks/purples/blues/greens
  169, 172–3
  in small spaces 75
  streamlined bathrooms 51,
  63–4
  using for different effects
  172–3
  white 38–9, 63, 109, 150,
  169–70
  yellows/oranges/reds 166–9
concrete 39, 163
  basin 108–9
  coloured 48
contemporary style 55
Corian R 104, 127
cork flooring 64, 158
crossbar taps 114–15, 116
cupboards/cabinets 124–5,
  128–31, 147
  built-in 20

disguised 52
faux 22
fitting 27
illuminating 100
knobs/handles 124
mirrored doors 52,
  135–6
in small spaces 75, 78
streamlined 63
see also display
curtains, draped 41

D

day beds 18, 131–3
decking/planking 23, 61–2,
  68, 75, 158–9
decoration 144–55
  indulgent 42, 48
  minimalist 51
  streamlined 62
dentist's/barber's chair 132
Design & Form 104
dimmer switches 58–61, 96,
  100
disabilities, planning around
  14–17, 113
display 174–81
  glass/china/shells 178–9
  shapes/colours/textures
  176
doors:
  bi-fold 83
  dividing space with 62–3,
  91
  pivoting 76, 83–4
  planning considerations 21,
  27–8, 78
downlighters 46, 96–8, 99
drainage/waste outlets 24, 31,
  34, 66–7
  baths 120
  spa/massage types 107
  centrally located 50–1
  handbasins 116–17
  shower area 46, 82, 84, 89
dressing rooms 23–4, 44
dressing tables 44, 132, 133
duckboards 64
DuPont 104

E

elderly:
  planning considerations
  14–16, 78, 113
electrics:
  appliances 121
  infrared sensors 56
  planning 17, 19
  professional installation 53
  see also safety
encaustic tiles 152
en suite rooms 18, 19, 62, 69,
  133
  adding shower cubicle 87
  disguising fixtures 62–3
equipment 94–103
  for small spaces 75–7
  see also fixtures and fittings
exercise/keep-fit facilities
  17–18
extractor fans 63, 98, 121

F

fabrics/upholstery 47–8
  planning considerations 18,
  132, 180
fibreboard 150
Ficore 104
fitting and installing 27–34
  height of items 27
fixtures and fittings 104–13
  mix and match 41
  showers 89, 89
  see also individual items
floor plans 14
floors/flooring 156–65
  hard 163–5
  non-slip 14, 87
  small spaces 68, 75
  streamlined rooms 62, 63–4
  textured coverings 20
  varying levels 24–5, 62, 150
  water damage/rot 28, 31
  weight considerations 24,
  32, 48
  see also under stone/
  marble/slate; wood
flower displays 176–7, 178,
  181

G

glass 148–9
  bricks 22, 53
  frosted 42
  handbasins 39, 42, 61, 65,
  110, 111
  reinforced/safety 39, 82, 83
  showers 89
  streamlined rooms 64
  tiles 152
grab rails 14, 17
Gray, Eileen 61
Grohtec Special Fittings
  range 56

H

handbasins 20, 39, 42, 61,
  65, 108–11, 124–7
  corner-fitting 77
  double 18, 20, 21, 41, 54,
  56
  freestanding 28, 110–11,
  131, 180
  installing antique 31
  metal 54, 55, 58–9, 108,
  111
  period-style 40, 42, 48
  position and height 27
  screening 22
  for small spaces 77, 78–9
  wall-mounted 14, 21,
  72, 77, 108–11, 147
heating 121–23
  combined with lighting
  98
  steel bathroom 56
  underfloor 24, 28, 42,
  63–4, 90
  wet rooms 90
hoist seat 17
Hot Spring radiator 121
Huster, Frank 39, 55